KT-431-839

Invitation to
THEOLOGY

INVITATION SERIES

Invitation to Medicine	Douglas Black
Invitation to Mathematics	John Bowers
Invitation to Theology	David Brown
Invitation to Philosophy	Martin Hollis
Invitation to Linguistics	Richard Hudson
Invitation to Social Work	Bill Jordan
Invitation to Industrial Relations	Tom Keenoy
Invitation to Statistics	Gavin Kennedy
Invitation to Teaching	Trevor Kerry
Invitation to Engineering	Eric Laithwaite
Invitation to Politics	Michael Laver
Invitation to Management	Peter Lawrence
Invitation to Astronomy	J. and S. Mitton
Invitation to Archaeology	Philip Rahtz
Invitation to Law	A. W. B. Simpson
Invitation to Economics	David Whynes

Other titles in preparation

Invitation to Anthropology	Maurice Bloch
Invitation to Nursing	June Clark
Invitation to Psychology	Philip Johnson-Laird

230
B877i

Invitation to
THEOLOGY

David Brown

15523

BASIL BLACKWELL

Copyright © David Brown 1989

First published 1989

Basil Blackwell Ltd
108 Cowley Road, Oxford, OX4 1JF, UK

Basil Blackwell Inc.
3 Cambridge Center
Cambridge, Massachusetts 02142, USA

All rights reserved. Except for the quotation of short passages for the purposes of criticism and review, no part of this publication may be reproduced, stored in a retrieval system, or transmitted, in any form or by any means, electronic, mechanical, photocopying, recording or otherwise, without the prior permission of the publisher.

Except in the United States of America, this book is sold subject to the condition that it shall not, by way of trade or otherwise, be lent, re-sold, hired out, or otherwise circulated without the publisher's prior consent in any form of binding or cover other than in which it is published and without a similar condition including this condition being imposed on the subsequent purchaser.

British Library Cataloguing in Publication Data

A CIP catalogue record for this book is available from the British Library.

Library of Congress Cataloging in Publication Data

Brown, David, 1948 June 1–
Invitation to theology / David Brown.
p.   cm. — (Invitation series)
Bibliography: p.
Includes index.
ISBN 0-631-16473-1
ISBN 0-631-16474-X (pbk.)
1. Theology.   I. Title.   II. Series.
BR118.B76   1990
230—dc19   89-31172
                                                      CIP

Typeset in 11½ on 12 pt Bembo
by Times Graphics
Printed in Great Britain by Billing & Sons Ltd, Worcester

Contents

Sept 90 NPH Bolton £6.08

Acknowledgements

My manuscript had the benefit of comments and criticisms from well over thirty individuals in schools, parishes and university. I trust that I may be allowed without offence to single out those who gave most aid. I am most grateful to pupils in the Lower Sixth at Dame Alice Harpur School, Bedford, for their detailed comments on the text. Much appreciated too were the lively discussion and pointers for improvement which emerged from those undergraduates at my own college of Oriel who participated in a weekly discussion of the material during Michaelmas Term 1988. But by far my greatest debt is undoubtedly to three teachers of religious studies in English schools, Paul Keyte, Margaret Laird and Christopher O'Neill. Their insistence that everything should be readily intelligible to their pupils has resulted in numerous changes to the text. Christopher O'Neill in particular took enormous care to ensure a more readable style than my own tendency towards Latinate constructions. Thanks is also due to Sue Martin for her great skill in copy editing. Apart from a very few exceptions when I have offered my own translation, quotations from the Bible are all either from the Authorized Version or from the Jerusalem Bible.

Introduction

Attitudes and Aims

Attitudes

So much misunderstanding exists about the nature of theology or religious studies that it might seem foolhardy to have accepted a request to write a book with a title like *Invitation to Theology*. But on the contrary, that very fact seemed a good reason for writing it: for so many of the reasons that make people suspicious of it are unfounded, based on false perceptions of what the subject is trying to achieve. Once these are overcome, then it is able to emerge as the truly fascinating and exciting subject that it really is.

The word 'theological' is in current English sometimes used as a term of abuse, to indicate some over-technically abstract or abstruse point that is not really worth discussing. How many angels can dance on the head of a pin might be an example, though even in the heyday of medieval scholasticism this issue was in fact never discussed. Of course it cannot be denied that there are such issues, for example arguments about whether the Spirit proceeds from the Father or from the Father and the Son (the so-called Filioque in the Nicene Creed that was one of the causes of the split between eastern and western Christianity in 1054). To the outsider such questions must inevitably appear trivial in the extreme, and the reader will probably be relieved to learn that I have no intention of discussing them here. But the important point to note is that the reason why they might conceivably be important can only be ascertained by entering into the spirit of a particular religious tradition and discovering what it values and why. For theology is not about picking up a number of facts which can be held in isolation, like the dates of the reigns of the Kings of England; it involves seeing interrelations between interlocking ideas and link-ups with a particular way of life before real understanding can be reached.

This point applies just as much to the Bible. I have known even highly educated dons at Oxford announce their intention of reconsidering Christianity by re-reading the entire Bible, from Genesis onwards. At that rate they are unlikely to get beyond the tedium of Leviticus! But the serious point I am trying to make is that the Bible, just as much as Christian doctrine, is something intended for community use and not just for individuals; and so, if you want to understand either Judaism or Christianity, you will need to learn how they use their sacred documents, which may be very different from either how they appear to you or from what they were originally intended to mean. Thus in all the main-line churches certain parts of the Bible are in effect a closed book and are never read in public worship. Nor does this apply only to the Old Testament. One is unlikely ever to hear anything from Revelation 6–20, with its strange vision of the End, which I remember as a child being told by a devout teacher must have been written by someone under the influence of hallucinogenic drugs. Fundamentalism, of course, conceives of itself very differently, with everything equally the inspired word of God, but in practice here too considerable modifications occur, with some of the more savage injunctions of the Old Testament seen as a temporary dispensation superseded by the new order in Christ. Likewise Judaism does not regard all of the Old Testament as of equal worth or importance. The Torah ('instruction' or 'law' – the first five books of the Bible) is given a similar prominence in worship to that accorded to the Gospels in Christianity, whereas of the other two sections of their Bible only certain selected excepts from the Prophets are ever heard as readings, while the third category, the Writings, are almost never heard.

I have laboured this point because western society is very individualistic in almost all its attitudes and if this is carried over into the study of religion it will inevitably distort one's perspective. Indeed, arguably Christianity itself is in large part to blame for this: for, more than any other religion, it has shaped western society, but it is also far more orientated towards doctrine and ideas than any other religion. Thus, though Judaism does have a minimal creed in the *Shema* (based on Deuteronomy 6:4), it is very much more a shared way of living than a system of ideas, and this is equally true of Hinduism, which is unintelligible except in terms of a total pattern of social existence.

It is precisely because understanding a religion means some sort of involvement with it in this way that some educationalists have questioned whether theology is properly an academic subject at all, and why others have instead seen the task as the dispassionate examination from outside of all religions, which is the rationale sometimes given for the preferred term, Religious Studies. But the truth of course is that all art subjects, not just theology, require a degree of empathy if any sort of deep appreciation of what is involved is to be achieved. Thus to revert to my earlier example of the dates of the reigns of the Kings of England, you would still have no appreciation of what the office really entailed until you had entered sympathetically into different aspirations current at different periods of English history, all very different from Britain's current model of constitutional monarchy. The good historian in effect temporarily suspends judgement and tries to feel and think how the people then felt and thought, so that he can properly understand what hopes and fears motivated them.

That is why it does not seem to me a matter of any great importance what we call the subject we are about to investigate. Rather, what matters is the attitude with which we approach it. These days the term 'theology' tends to be used of the study of a particular religion in detail or, more narrowly still, of the doctrines of that particular religion. By contrast 'religious studies' usually have as an essential element in their course the comparative study of at least one other religion as well as Christianity, together with reference to the attempts of the social sciences, particularly sociology and psychology to account for the phenomenon of religion. In what follows I shall attempt to show why both approaches to the subject can be found challenging and exciting. The majority of my examples will be drawn from Christianity, and so in that sense the book can be seen as an introduction to Christian theology. But there is perhaps a deeper sense in which it is also an introduction to religious studies. Each of the chapters is concerned with a particular religious phenomenon, for example the study of a religion's past or the study of a religious text. Yet, whichever approach the reader finds more interesting, I must return to my basic point that subordinate to both is the need for the right kind of attitude.

This is very different from saying that religious belief is required. Indeed, belief can sometimes be a barrier in preventing imaginative engagement with those of very different religious traditions. But equally anyone who thinks of those with belief as fools is unlikely to make much progress in understanding, just as anyone contemptuously dismissive of the values of medieval society is unlikely to make much progress in understanding it.

Aims

To help achieve that goal of understanding, what follows is divided into four chapters. The first deals with 'The Nature of Religion' and in particular some of the kinds of questions that the religious quest is seeking to answer. This must come first because unless we get that right, we are likely to labour under major misapprehensions about what it is that the various religions are trying to achieve. At this stage we shall look at the earliest form of theology, the production of myths, and I shall try to show how, far from being mere primitive superstition, they represent the work of intelligent beings like ourselves and in fact have a clear counterpart in some modern novel writing. Most religions, however, believe that religion is not just a matter of man's search for God but also of God's search for man, of his disclosing or revealing himself, and so the following chapter on 'The Bible's Theologians' examines one particular such revelation and how study of such a text might proceed. But, as the title of the chapter indicates, it seems to me that here too a proper understanding will only be reached once

4

it is appreciated that, however we suppose the divine hand to be at work, equally at work is the hand of the individual theologian. That hand, however, did not cease with the production of the sacred text. All the major religions have continued to change and develop over their history, and so chapter 3 'A Changing Church', is devoted to examining some specific examples of what study of this historical dimension might involve. Finally, the last chapter gives some illustrations of theology at work today.

Though the book is short we will thus have covered the history of theology from its earliers beginnings to the present day; and not only that, for I hope to illustrate in the process most of the other disciplines upon which theology and religious studies rely, including history, literary criticism, sociology, anthropology and philosophy. Such a range is unfortunately necessary even within the compass of such a short book if an accurate reflection is to be given of the way in which theology is studied in the academic context of universities and seminaries. Personally I find that range one of the very factors that makes theology so exciting, but it is not hard to see why it might appear initially rather daunting to readers. So to alleviate that impression, I have introduced two features in what follows which will, I hope, considerably ease their path.

First, the book abounds in examples. So, though I do ask the reader to think hard, the illustrations should help in focusing on what exactly is required. The German nineteenth-century philosopher, Friedrich Nietzsche once said that there are no facts, only interpretations. That is an exaggeration, but all arts subjects, not just theology, do involve a considerable amount of interpretation. That is to say, assessment of the facts is involved ('facts' which may themselves be interpretations) and so, while one can talk about degrees of plausibility, there is seldodm a sure-fire way of giving a knock-down argument to show that all relevant considerations have been taken into account. Yet many scholars (perhaps because they have invested so much time in producing their theories) often write as though matters were now absolutely certain. This then produces a complete misunderstanding of the subject on the part of the student, who supposes it is just a matter of learning all the latest facts. It is to guard against any such notion that throughout the book I have given illustrations of the way in which scholarly opinion can change, not necessarily through new facts being discovered but through some already existing factor now being given more (or less) weight. A new significance can be discovered thanks to a change in interpretative framework. Indeed, this can sometimes happen to entire subjects. Think for instance of the decline of classical studies in our own century or the great expansion of the study of Scottish history in the past twenty years. It is not that new facts have been discovered. Rather, Scottish history has acquired a new significance because of the rise of Scottish nationalism. Similar changes and reassessments occur in theology. One might take as examples the latest anthropological reassessments of myth, or the New Testament scholars' discovery of strongly theologian motivations behind the writing of the Gospels, or more recent attempts to explain the rise of interest in witchcraft in seventeenth-century England, all of which are discussed in subsequent chapters.

Of course the reader must not jump from these remarks to the opposite extreme of supposing that everything is totally relative. It is still possible to choose between interpretative frameworks – some are simpler than others, some explain more, some are more easily made compatible with what else we know, and so forth. All I am trying to ensure is that my readers think for themselves, and do not rely even on me; the illustrations are there to begin your thinking, not end it.

But of course I realize that many of these new facts and new interpretations can be traumatic for the religious believer. He or she may hitherto have thought of the Bible as unqualifiedly 'the word of God' and so without error, or may have supposed that doctrine is unaffected by the society in which it is set. Society in general despises such simple faith, little realizing that it is just as naive about the total objectivity of science – think for instance of the somersault science has undergone from its very mechanistic views in the nineteenth century to the indeterminacy of twentieth-century quantum physics. So I certainly do not share this contempt for the fundamentalist;

indeed, much of the blame for fundamentalism seems to me to lie with the academic world. So concerned is it to display objectivity and impartiality that it often seems reluctant to specify how God might be involved in the process at all. Yet theology means 'the study of God'. This then is the explanation for the second feature which I have introduced to ease the reader's path, the fact that I have tried to indicate throughout how the new and often startling conclusions being thrown up by academic theology can none the less be integrated into a continuing pattern and framework of religous belief. The world and the Bible are very different from what we once thought, but, far from this being a threat to the Church, it seems to me to have inherent within it the potential for an enormous enrichment of its life. Of course that will mean change, but as Chapter 3 amply illustrates, the Church has always been in the process of change. So there need be no reason for anxiety or fear about what follows.

All writing is of course done from some perspective or another, and in this case, as should now be obvious, I write as a believing Christian. But it would be a sad day for the world if authors could only engage the interest of those with whom they agreed; and whether successful or not, certainly my intention in what follows has been to show how the issues concerned can become fascinating to those of any faith or none.

1

The Nature of Religion

If so short a book as this is to avoid superficiality, it will be necessary to concentrate on one particular religion. That is one reason why the three subsequent chapters concentrate on Christianity. But first in this chapter I shall attempt to characterize the nature of religion in general, with examples drawn from both primitive religions and other world religions. What is it to raise religious questions? What is it to offer a religious perspective as a response? In seeking to answer such questions, I want to examine in turn three types of theologizing, starting with the most primitive and most misunderstood of all, religion as myth; continuing with the more abstract form of thinking in which religion functions as a search for meaning; and finally looking at that search from the alternative perspective of it really being God's search for us, when it takes the form of religion as revelation. At each stage I shall also try to assess the relevance of a related discipline – in turn anthropology, psychology and sociology. Consideration of philosophy will be delayed until the final chapter.

RELIGION AS MYTH

Anthropology

In ordinary English the word 'myth' is used almost synonymously with 'falsehood' or at most is taken to mean 'legend', a good yarn but without truth. Anthropology particularly concerns itself with the study of primitive peoples, and for a long time anthropologists were scarcely any more complimentary about the major role myth plays in the life of such peoples. E. B. Tylor saw it as a barbaric form of mentality, J. G. Frazer identified sympathetic magic as its chief characteristic, while Lucien Lévy-Bruhl spoke of it as belonging to a 'prelogical' stage of mankind's development. However, increasingly since the Second World War a more positive estimate has been given. Some anthropologists like the Frenchman Claude Lévi-Strauss are still essentially reductive, insisting that the myths *only* tell us something about the social setting of those who use them; but this view can easily be complemented by eminent reseachers of the calibre of the Romanian scholar Mircea Eliade who spent a large part of his working life at the University of Chicago. His writings are replete with discussions of the *religious* significance of myth.

But, whether one takes Lévi-Strauss or Eliade as typical, there can be no doubt about the transformation of attitudes. Myth is now seen as an alternative mode of thinking to conceptual discourse, and just as intelligent. By conceptual discourse I mean our ability to use abstract ideas. Make a list of abstract nouns (not things) and you will quickly see what is meant – thankfulness, omniscience, intention, aesthetics and so on. Because it is very difficult to retain abstract ideas in one's head, this type of thinking really only becomes possible with the invention of writing, which allows you (as perhaps with this book) to keep looking back at particular sentences until you have completely grasped them. By contrast, a society that is still relying exclusively on oral communication must proceed rather differently. If you can only hear them once, it is easier to retain what is said if it is presented in the form of vivid metaphors, striking images and good stories. It is precisely at this point that myth comes into its own.

Myth is not *just* a different way of thinking; it also follows a different set of rules. With conceptual thinking there are rules of logic, what follows logically from what. (If you are omniscient then it follows that you will know that I am typing this sentence at the moment, and am not using a word-processor.) On the other hand, myth is like metaphor: you can say two apparently contradictory things, and yet both of them be true. Once upon a time young men used to call their sweethearts things like 'honey' and 'rose'. In so doing they were using metaphors, both of which could be true of the girl concerned (she was sweet and pretty), though literally she was neither honey nor a rose.

It is important to be aware of this distinction because it helps to explain the apparently chaotic character of myth. According to the rules of ordinary conceptual thought you may expect a myth to be true literally, whereas its truth lies elsewhere at a non-literal level. Two myths may also *appear* to conflict at the literal level without either really undermining the other. Myths are constantly being altered during their history. It is partly because, as story-tellers know the world over, if a story is to appear fresh, it has to be told in a slightly modified way. But it also because since the value of the story lies in its symbolic and not its literal sense there is no reason why it should not be adapted to make a rather different symbolic point. So for instance in Greek mythology we find Orestes in Homer's *Odyssey* being held up as a model of filial piety because he killed his mother and her lover without qualms, whereas by the time of the tragedian Aeschylus the qualms have become one of the main points of the story.

As that example illustrates, myth did continue into the age of writing, but, as the history of the classical world indicates, it gradually gave way under attack in the West to conceptual thinking, though as we shall see it has survived in the East in Hinduism to this day with much of its force still intact. Greece's two most famous philosophers, Plato and Aristotle, both attacked myths. The former condemned the immoral way in which they presented the gods, while the latter spoke contemptuously of the 'theologians' who composed such stories. Yet Plato did seem to appreciate the power of myth, because he thought it important to produce some alternative myths for the ideal society he depicts in *The Republic*. But really once conceptual thinking had taken a firm hold on society, the future of myth was doomed. Anyone now hearing the story translates its meaning into conceptual terms, and so the myth in effect becomes redundant, whereas when it exists on its own as the only way of thinking then all we can do is, as

10

it were, think pictorially and laterally, moving from image to image, and from metaphor to metaphor.

We may find the idea of pictorial thinking very strange, but it is in fact probably how we also first began to think as children. Indeed, psychologists like Bruno Bettelheim tell us that this is the major source from which fairy tales derive their power. For instance, the tale of 'Jack the Giant-Killer' is enjoyed by children despite all its gruesome incidents because by analogy the child can infer that it too, like Jack, can survive very well amidst all the nasty threats of tall creatures like giants and grown-ups.

To appreciate the religious import of myth one must continue this task of trying to think oneself into a very different world from our own adult culture. Today we tend to compartmentalize our lives with religion as merely one compartment. Religion implies going to church on Sunday, reading the Bible and so forth, but not work at the office or washing one's car. But to the ancient mind there were no such distinctions. Everything in the world partook of the divine, everything was sacred. So for instance the original Olympic Games (founded 776 BC) was a religious festival, and indeed one ancient historian, Peter Brown, has suggested that it is as if a sports correspondent sent to report on the Olympics today should instead discover himself in the midst of the Holy Week ceremonies at Seville. In other words, athletic prowess was seen as a divine gift and treated accordingly. So too was all creativity. The famous tragedies and comedies of ancient Athens were all performed at the religious festival of Dionysia and the comedies could even include jokes about the gods. Again, many in the opening procession would be carrying a model of an erect phallus, not as a joke, nor because they were promiscuous, but because the creativity of sexuality was also seen as a divine gift. In short, all their experience of the world was seen as partaking in the divine, and so nothing could be divorced from the religious dimension.

But precisely because the world has so many different aspects, this was taken to imply a plurality of gods. Some classical scholars (for example, Vernant) suggest that we think of the gods of Greece as more like powers than persons, and it

11

is certainly the case that even the same god could be seen as having contradictory aspects, with the god under one epithet viewed as favourable to the worshipper and under another hostile. But, however we interpret the gods, it is certainly the case that the myths were there to evoke this underlying sacred reality to the world and to indicate how best to come to terms with it. For example, the point of the story of the sexually chaste Hippolytus punished by the goddess of love, Aphrodite, is that one ignores the divine creation of sexuality at one's peril. And the myth of Prometheus stealing fire from the gods indicates man's position as neither god not beast; unlike the beasts he possess fire, but unlike the gods he does not do so of right.

Myth in the Bible

Though there are examples of pure myth in the Bible, most obviously in the story of Adam and Eve, in its present form the Bible belongs mainly to a post-mythological way of thinking. At the same time it is important that one should appreciate that its thinking is often still transitional. Thus it was only once Christianity moved out into the late classical world that it acquired completely abstract concepts with which to discuss its faith. The biblical writers still thought in concrete terms and images. What is vital for a correct understanding of the biblical text is awareness that many of the rules of mythological thinking continued to be in force, so far as its images are concerned. Thus, as we shall observe in chapter 2, they do not share our distinction between historical fact and symbolic fact. For them, both could be written about in much the same kind of way.

But more of this later. In the meantime let me simply give one illustration of this half-way house: the opening chapter of Genesis. Although the Bible opens in this mythological way, central rather to the Old Testament view of God is the idea of God's action in history and his involvement with a particular people. The theme of creation is seldom to be found in any explicit form, and in fact the Bible's opening story of the creation is a late response to, and adaptation of, an already existing

12

Babylonian myth. This is important to note because, though most primitive peoples do have some form of creation myth, it would be quite wrong to suggest that puzzling about how the world began is what makes them 'theologians'. Such a view would equate theology with primitive science. Of course religion did sometimes function like that, as with the use of demons to explain the existence of physical illness, but to see that as central would be to misunderstand totally the aims of religious thinking. What was being explored through myth was a meaningful framework in terms of which one could intelligibly relate to the world and respond to it. Thus, in so far as the question of creation was raised, it was raised as a way of considering what the world now is like, not what it was like when it began. So even in creation myths the interest was not in causal explanations but in a search for meaning, a framework in terms of which life could be lived.

This is beautifully illustrated by that opening chapter, and the alterations the author makes. Scholars call him P because he is believed to have been a priestly editor (or editors) of the Pentateuch (the first five books of the Bible), writing about 500 BC, who sometimes incorporates his sources unchanged, sometimes adds material of his own, and sometimes – as in this case – reworks earlier pagan accounts. The original Babylonian myth, called *Enuma Elish*, had presented a rather negative view. The world's creation was due to conflict, a battle between the gods. P retains various mythological elements such as the divisions of days and God 'resting' on the seventh day, but at the same time removes all the negative import of the myth. The defeated goddess Tiamat, the chaos monster out of whom the cosmos was created by the god Marduk, survives only as the *tehom*, the related Hebrew word for the unformed watery chaos. The point being made is that the world is good (repeatedly affirmed in the declaration 'and God saw that it was good') and not a battleground of the gods. Indeed, so little is the writer concerned to offer a causal explanation that no account is given of how the *tehom* came into existence, and we must await that for several centuries until the apocryphal 2 Maccabees (7:28). Indeed, even well into the Christian era some of the Church Fathers, for example Justin Martyr and

Clement of Alexandria, still saw no need for a doctrine of divine creation out of nothing.

Our point can be carried further by observing that modern scholarship reveals that P has combined his account with an earlier version that begins at Genesis 2:4 in a way that indicates that causal explanation could not have been his primary aim. For once one compares the two chapters closely, the inconsistencies are clearly to be seen, with, for example, plants appearing later than man in the earlier account (2:19–20), or again woman being created separately from man (2:22) rather than simultaneously as in the later version (1:26–7). Either we have to say that P was a rather poor editor (in addition to producing his own material he introduced elements from sources known as J, E and D) or, surely more probably, we must recognize that for him such inconsistencies did not matter, because giving an account of the origins of the cosmos was not the objective with which he was writing. In other words, it was a matter of complete indifference to him when and how the plants arrived. What mattered was that they were good and part of an ordered, structured universe in which God had a plan and purpose for man.

I hasten to add that I am not denying that myths were sometimes invented to give an explanation. Indeed, there is a whole category of them concerned with the explanation of the origin of the names of peoples and places. They are called aetiological myths, and examples can be found in the Bible, as in the story in Genesis 32: 24ff of Jacob (Hebrew = 'the supplanter') wrestling with God and being renamed Israel (Hebrew = 'perseverer with God'). But even here the reason why J chooses to tell the story is ultimately theological, that Jacob who had cheated his elder brother of his rightful blessing has at last won through by his perseverance and been blessed by God. The mythical story is merely seen as symbolizing this.

Myth in Hinduism

Myth is of course only one way of searching for meaning and not one pursued today in the modern western world, but it is worth delaying a little longer over the concept because it does have, I think, at least two contemporary counterparts, in the still living mythological tradition of Hinduism and in some forms of novel writing in the western world.

Hinduism is of all the major world religions certainly the most difficult for the modern mind to come to terms with. It is all too easy to be dismissive and regard it in the same light as the pagan cults which populated the ancient classical world before the arrival of Christianity. Certainly it has if anything a richer tradition of legends of the gods, especially as represented in its two great epics, the *Ramayana* and *Mahabharata*. Like the Greek god Zeus, Vishnu is believed to have appeared on earth in animal form, and even when such a descent or *avatar* takes human form the god does not behave entirely morally. Thus the seventh avatar of Vishnu was as Krishna who plays the part of a mischievous youth, good at the flute, who has various amorous adventures. Nowadays such a story tends to be read allegorically as representing devotion to this god. Tales of the other main Hindu god, Shiva, are often similarly re-interpreted. Yet, just as in the classical world, alongside this mythology there existed strongly monotheistic expressions of faith as in the Stoic philosopher Cleanthes' famous *Hymn to Zeus*, so to a very much greater degree is this true of Hinduism. Major deities like Vishnu and Shiva are seen (at least by educated Hindus) as simply aspects of the one all-encompassing divine reality that is Brahman. Some of the myths, most obviously perhaps the *Bhagavadgita* section of the *Mahabharata*, can easily be interpreted in terms of this search for meaning which I mentioned earlier. It is the *Bhagavadgita* which has produced the modern *bhakti* or devotion cults to Krishna which play such a major role in contemporary Hinduism. From its story has come the inspiration for viewing loving devotion as a higher mode of life than the search for intellectual enlightenment or the pursuit of correct action. Again, consider the prayer many Hindus say on getting up in the morning: 'O Prithivi, consort of Vishnu, you who wear a sari in the form of the Seven Seas and have mountains for ornaments, forgive us for touching you with our feet.' The mythology is there in a subordinate role to enhance the sense of reverence due to all the world which is suffused with the divine.

But equally we must guard against the danger of supposing

that all Hindu mythology can be interpreted in this way. Some seems to be there for no deeper reason than a natural love of story-telling, and if it be asked why myth and more typically religious concerns can continue to exist side by side without any sustained attempt to disentangle them, the answer must surely lie in a different attitude to history. The three strongly monotheistic religions of Judaism, Christianity and Islam all stem from ancient Israel's concern with a God involved in history, in terms of which it was important to distinguish what he had and had not done in the world: whereas in the Indian culture of Hinduism fact and fiction were both alike relativized as *maya* (illusion) in relation to deeper but unseen realities such as Brahman. It is this fact which makes Hinduism the most tolerant of all the world religions, with Christianity seen as just another aspect of the manifestation of the divine, with the question of its historicity, so central to traditional Christian self-understanding, relegated to a peripheral issue.

Novels as a form of myth

But, if myth as a search for meaning is still a living force in modern India, this is not generally so in the western world. The nearest western equivalent is that type of allegorical or symbolic novel where surface details of plot and character enshrine deeper ideas or issues. Sometimes the religious content is very explicit, as in Michele Roberts's *The Wild Girl* (1984), with her attempt to retell the story of Mary Magdalene in a way in which she can be made more directly relevant to contemporary feminist concerns; or again, as in Michel Tournier's *The Four Wise Men* (1982), with its story of a fourth wise man (an Indian) in search of the perfect recipe for Turkish Delight, who in fact never sets his eyes on Jesus but has his perceptions transformed in the course of his stay in Palestine. But usually the more successful novels are those which are less explicit. Perhaps I may give a number of examples at random.

William Golding, winner of the Nobel Prize for Literature, is someone whose religious commitment is strong, but who lets the reader discover this meaning for himself. It is possible to read him just as a good story-teller, but certainly more is intended. In *Lord of the Flies* (1954) Golding sets himself the task of drawing a portrait of human nature which is truer to life than the naive and prettified unrealities of R. M. Ballantyne's classic account of human nature left to itself on a desert island, *Coral Island* (1857). The stalwart and decent chaps, Ralph, Jack and Peterkin of Ballantyne's book, become in Golding's version the respective leaders of rival gangs of prep-school boys who quickly leave behind the constraints of civilization and degenerate into barbarism, even killing one another.

Thus it is no accident that the novel was entitled *Lord of the Flies* – the commonly accepted English translation for one of the New Testament titles for Satan, Beelzebub; for the underlying theme is the power of evil that lies even within the most innocent of us. This story of the slide into corruption of young boys stranded in the apparent paradise of a desert island can thus easily be read as a retelling of the myth of the Garden of Eden, with the same point being made. Adam and Eve too had been innocent but envy and greed likewise drove them to fight among themselves, with Adam blaming Eve and Eve the serpent, and one of their sons murdering the other not long thereafter. Golding's story, just like the Adam and Eve myth, is thus concerned with what theologians have come to label as the problem of 'original sin' – the fact that, though created innocent and free, we have the potential for realizing tremendous forces for evil as well as for good, and the consequent problem of how we are to deal with this. Two of his other novels present the alternatives, as Golding sees them, very starkly. On the one hand, there is our power to self-destruct totally in the pursuit of egoism, as happens with *Pincher Martin* (1956). On the other, there is the release of seeking forgiveness from something larger than ourselves as epitomized in the story of *The Spire* (1964), where Jocelin comes to the realization that his attempt to build a vast spire for his cathedral has simply been an exercise in vanity and self-aggrandisement. Through recognition of this fact he is enabled to seek and obtain forgiveness, symbolized by his dying vision of the apple-tree: though still rooted to the earth, it now soars to the sky. No longer was it just something from which forbidden fruit had been plucked (as with the tree in the Garden of Eden);

the very recognition of the fruit *as* forbidden meant that a new life of inner peace could at last develop.

Original sin and the need for forgiveness are two major themes of Christian theology. So too is atonement (reconciliation) and here one can detect an echo in many contemporary novels, including those written by non-believers. In Ken Kesey's *One Flew Over the Cuckoo's Nest* (1962) it is only thanks to the hero, McMurphy, that the inmates of a mental hospital recover their own sense of identity and self-respect, but this is at the cost of McMurphy's own sanity when he is given a compulsory lobotomy. It seems likely that Kesey intended some religious allusion, for one does find an occasional piece of significant symbolism. For example, the number of followers who break out with McMurphy from the hospital is given as twelve; and during the lobotomy the wires being attached to his head are described in the manner of a crown of thorns. But, however that may be, the general theme is certainly that of atonement (literally making at one), and of how reconcilation and release for others need so often to be bought at the price of an innocent's life. Christianity of course sees this supremely in the case of the death of Christ.

But the issue does not just raise itself narrowly with respect to that one death. Indeed, there is no shortage of other novels to which we might refer. But what is particularly interesting to observe is the way in which the novel can itself be a vehicle for theological debate. Thus if the Billy Budd of Herman Melville's original novel or Benjamin Britten's opera typifies the innocent victim as bearer of this role, Graham Greene's novels have been a recurring challenge to consider whether the cult of purity has not led to an undervaluing of the flawed individual's ability to play this role. He even raises the question whether the flawed act may not itself sometimes be an instrument of atonement. (The obvious example of the former is the whisky priest in *The Power and the Glory* (1940) while of several examples of the latter one might mention Scobie's suicide in *The Heart of the Matter* (1948). It is perhaps therefore not surprising that for long Greene found himself out of favour with his adopted denomination, the Roman Catholic Church.

18

RELIGION AS MEANING

So far we have been examining the way in which religious answers have been sought through pictures, through mythological ways of thinking. I want now to turn to explicitly conceptual thinking, but still not to highly abstract forms of thought. Rather, I shall take types of reflection with which almost everyone must be familiar. Two in particular may be singled out, the first of which I shall label 'the cosmological experience', while the second is concerned with the more negative aspects of existence, suffering, anger and doubt, and how they relate to religious belief. Philosophers have of course had much to say on these issues, but, as mentioned earlier, I shall delay consideration of the relevance of philosophy to theology until the final chapter.

The cosmological experience

Some readers may already be familiar with one of the traditional arguments for God's existence, known as the cosmological argument. This maintains that the only adequate explanation for all the causal processes in the world (the cosmos) must lie in that which is itself uncaused. This we call God, the source of all that is and thus himself dependent on nothing. But long before philosophers usurped the discussion there existed an intuition among many people that somehow everything and everybody is part of a greater whole which is underpinned by an even deeper reality. They felt that it was to this underlying unity that aspects of their experience pointed. It is this experiential conviction which I want to label 'the cosmological experience'.

Radical evil, forgiveness and atonement are of course not essentially religious themes. In theory at least they could be discussed in a purely secular context, but it is interesting to observe how seldom this is the case. For example, they play no significant role in contemporary philosophical discussion. Why then do they bulk so large in the religious consciousness? The answer may well have much to do with the religious desire for a unified view of life. Radical evil after all presents the greatest challenge to such a possibility, while forgiveness and atonement both suggest the feasibility of its realization, though at a cost. It certainly seems true that all world religions seek such a unified and holistic picture. In the theistic religions this is still further reinforced by the notion of a creator God, where the whole world is seen as having a single point or *raison d'être* in that one Being. In practice, that religious search for unity finds expression even in much polytheistic religion. The tendency is either for only the local god to be worshipped (a practice known as henotheism), or for the division of tasks between the gods to be carefully demarcated, with perhaps a presiding god to ensure that the conventions are maintained.

It is perhaps factors such as this that explain the continuing popularity of the cosmological argument for God's existence rather than any technical success it might have when presented purely as a philosophical argument. For what seems to attract the religious mind is not any certainty the argument might bring but its insistence that everything that exists can be brought under a single all-encompassing framework. I use the word 'framework' rather than 'explanation' because the latter term seems to encapsulate the philosopher's mind rather than the purely religious element in the notion. What is important is that God as the source of everything and not himself dependent on anything can give a unity to the world and our experience of it, despite all its disparateness. Of course, there may be no such ultimate unity, but the religious are not alone in seeking such an account. Marxist materialism offers a similar all-encompassing account of life in society and the world. Nor do the similarities end at the intellectual level. It has often been noted that several of the trappings of religion have taken new shape in Marxist societies, as for instance in the use of the address 'comrade' or the huge portraits of leaders that until relatively recently were always carried in procession on major occasions and which seemed to fulfil a suspiciously similar role to that once performed by icons.

Friedrich Schleiermacher (d. 1834) is often described as the founder of modern Christian theology. In his writings the appeal to experience bulks large, and significantly it is to what we may call the cosmological experience that he makes most frequent appeal. He speaks of a feeling of 'absolute dependence' as central to religion, and draws from this a strongly unified perception of reality. The language is unfortunate and indeed led his contemporary G. W. F. Hegel (d.1831) to protest that it turned human beings into dogs, creatures of pure dependency and incapable of independent judgement. But that was not, I think, Schleiermacher's intention. What he wanted to stress was the radical contingency of the world, the way in which it might so easily have all been very different and indeed might not have existed at all. We only exist because of something other than ourselves, and that must inevitably evoke feelings of gratitude for being alive and, though of course it does not thereby follow that anyone exists who can be a suitable recipient of that thanks, it at least raises the possibility.

Gratitude is, of course, one of the incentives to worship. Awe is another. Beauty and mystery may or may not be closely allied, but certainly awe can be generated by phenomena as varied as a beautiful landscape or the sight of a new-born child. Nor does it seem to be the case that science necessarily does anything to destroy that sense of wonder and awe – surveys of academics have found that the proportion of religious believers is higher among scientists than in the arts subjects, not lower. Perhaps the explanation lies in a greater appreciation of the beauty of the detailed ordering of the universe, or perhaps the sense of mystery deepens with the realization that the more we come to know the less we completely understand, as one theory succeeds another, with Newton, for example, giving place to Einstein and so on.

Nor should we think of such experience being narrowly confined to those who participate in some form of community worship. For surveys done through Gallup and NOP polls in the United States and Britain indicate that a very much higher percentage of the population are prepared to claim religious experience than regularly attend church. Certainly the questions were deliberately vague, talking of 'awareness of a divine presence' or 'feeling as though one were very close to a powerful spiritual force'. But, if the figures are at all reliable, what they appear to indicate is that the religious quest is generated not only by the search for an overall unifying framework for life but also by belief in an awareness, however dim, of something corresponding to that search, and that this can exist independently and apart from any adherence to the claims of a revealed religion. The theistic religions of course believe that they have an explanation for such an awareness in the ubiquitous presence of God sustaining the world in existence. So, for example, Psalm 19 opens with the declaration that 'The heavens declare the glory of God; and the firmament showeth his handiwork', while in the Quran Allah declares: 'We created man. We know the promptings of his soul, and are closer to him that the vein of his neck.' However, the lack of correspondence between such claims and religious observance does suggest that, in the West at least, organized religion seriously fails to reflect in its worship the character of that experience.

Suffering, anger and doubt

Yet despite the wide extent of religious experience in the population at large, it remains the case that for many their experience is simply of the absence of God, or at any rate of his distance for most or even all of the time. Each of the theistic religions claim this barrier can be overcome because God has made us for communion with himself, though the journey may be long and the way dark. For religion too has had to come to terms with a dark side of the world, a side upon which many believe its claims founder, namely the problem of evil. Thus Judaism has both the figure of Job being urged by his wife to curse God for the undeserved suffering God has inflicted upon him and, more recently, all the horrors of the Holocaust. Christianity has as its central symbol Jesus Christ hanging on the Cross, crying: 'My God, my God, why hast thou forsaken me?' But only Buddhism has made the problem absolutely central to its entire perspective. 'Suffering I teach – and the way out of suffering', is how the Buddha summarized his message. The Buddha's enlightenment consisted in the discovery of the Four Noble Truths: that suffering is unavoidable, that suffering is caused by desire, that escape from such desire is supreme bliss (*nirvana*), and that it is through following the Buddha's Eightfold Path that such desire would be eliminated.

Obviously there is not the space here to discuss the relative merits of the various approaches of the different religions. Rather, I want to make two general points. First, far from religion failing to come to terms with evil, it has often been one of the motivating factors towards the religious quest, most obviously in the case of Buddhism. Here human beings have often felt the greatest need for meaning in their lives, and religions which see redemptive value in suffering or seek to reduce its importance can contribute to that quest But, secondly, it needs to be stressed that this has in no way led to a trivialization of suffering even in those eastern religions which take the latter course. Joseph Heller of *Catch 22* fame in a more recent novel, *God Knows* (1984), portrays King David upbraiding God in fairly crude terms for his treatment of him in the latter, more tragic part of his reign. The primary intention is comic, but whether Heller realizes it or not he is fully within the Old Testament tradition, as, for instance in the unrelieved gloom of the accusations levelled against God in Psalm 88. In fact even today hospital chaplains are fully aware of the need for people to rail against God before they can finally come to terms with their plight. So emotions that non-believers think incompatible with religious faith are in fact firmly embedded in the tradition. Indeed, not only is this true of anger against God; it is equally true of doubt. Enshrined in the Old Testament is the doubters' Bible, the Book of Ecclesiastes, while even the mystics of subsequent Christian centuries were to speak of their own 'dark night of the soul'. Doubt and anger too have their role to play in this all-encompassing religious perspective.

The psychological objection

But this very inclusiveness of religion, its apparent ability to deal with every situation, however wretched, is often turned against it to offer what is often thought to be a decisive objection to any form of religious belief. It is said that the only reason for people becoming religious is as an escape from harsh reality into the comforting reassurance of a divine protector. Sometimes this view gains a more respectable intellectual veneer by reference to Sigmund Freud's notion of God as the projection of a childhood authority, the Father-figure. For those outside theology and religion, such wisps of psychology are often the only way known in which psychology might be thought relevant to religion, just as the popular view might see sociology as providing clear evidence that one's religion is simply an accident of birth: born a Protestant, one ends up a Protestant, and so on for Catholics, Hindus or Jews. That knowledge of these two disciplines should be so narrowly confined is a pity, not only because the two types of objection are not particularly forceful, but also because the pyschology and sociology of religion have very much more important things to contribute to our understanding of religion.

It is, of course, false to suggest that religion is always comforting. It can lead to painful decisions and commitments, as for example under persecution. But, even were this always so, this would still not show it to be false, any more than the fact that belief in the love of parent or wife is comforting shows that that belief too is without foundation. Mooveover, it might be that God has so made us that, as Augustine puts it, 'our hearts are restless until they find rest in Thee'. Again, so far as the sociological objection is concerned, it is of course true that where one is born will affect what one believes, but this is true not just of religion but of very many of our beliefs (for example, our attitude to the status of women, or atheism itself in the western world) and, though social pressures are strong, this does not mean that we have no capacity to step outside them nor that there is no truth to be found once we take that step. Indeed, the increasing pluralism of western society means that our options are becoming more and more open.

At the end of this chapter I shall illustrate the positive use of sociology by the way in which it has deepened our under-standing of developments within Buddhism and Islam. This is of course in no way to suggest that the same kind of application cannot be made to Christianity. Indeed, perhaps the most famous early application of sociology to religion was Max Weber's thesis (in *The Protestant Ethic and the Spirit of Capitalism*, 1904) that it was certain kinds of theological attitudes within Protestantism that made possible the rapid advance of capitalism in northern Europe. Again, biblical scholars have recently shown much interest in the application of sociological techniques to the Bible, ranging from Norman Gottwald's Marxist analysis of the early settlement of Caanan in *Tribes of Yahweh* (1979) to Gerd Theissen's impressive presentation of the situation at the time of Jesus in his biographical novel *The Shadow of the Galilean* (1987).

Likewise psychology too has brought many positive benefits to the study of religion. Admittedly Freud gave a very negative verdict, describing religion in *The Future of an Illusion* (1928) as a 'universal obsessional neurosis', but it is important to recall that Freud represents only one of a number of schools of psychological thought. Other psychologists often give a much more positive evaluation. Recent American research has demonstrated that in general religious believers are less neurotic than the norm, and the other great genius of depth psychology, Carl Jung, spent much of his life trying to identify religious 'archetypes' or images common to our 'collective unconscious'; he even on one occasion went so far as to claim that none of his patients had been properly healed until they had acquired a religious outlook on life. Again, the so-called personalist psychologists (Gordon Allport, A.H. Maslow and Rollo May) have seen religion as a positive force in helping to produce a properly integrated personality, better able to achieve desired goals. Assessing the rival merits of such total accounts of human personality is no easy matter. Probably, as with the genesis of religious belief itself, it is a mistake to suppose that there is always one correct answer, rather than a great variety of different factors simultaneously playing their part.

Psychological research can impinge on religion not only on the level of general theory, but also with respect to specific case studies. Let me give just two examples. One researcher (Antoine Vergote) found that, despite the Christian use of the image of God as Father, the paternal qualities assigned to one's own father and to God bore little relation. Another (Allport) made the intriguing discovery in one of his studies that prejudice increases with the occasional practice of religion but then sharply declines the more devout one becomes. While the former offers reassurance that religious imagery is not too easily misunderstood, the latter would seem to present a challenge to religion to do something to rectify the situation. Indeed, many psychological studies are now being used by clergy to improve pastoral practice, as for example with studies of the psychology of bereavement or conversion.

In effect, such studies are being used to facilitate the religious quest for meaning. But with the exception of Buddhism all the major religions see themselves not just in terms of man's search for God but also, and indeed in most cases predominantly, in terms of God's search for man. For they all talk of God's revelation to man, and so it is to that question that we must next turn.

RELIGION AS REVELATION

Not long after the Soviet Union succeeded in putting the first man into space, the Soviet leader Nikita Krushchev commented: 'Our pilots have gone far into the sky and not found God anywhere there.' The remark is an interesting one, for it highlights the way in which God's relationship to the world is misunderstood, and with it the concept of revelation. God is envisaged almost as though he were an occasional visitor from outer space, rather in the manner of films like *2001* or the delightful *ET*. For this Christianity is in part to blame: so concerned has it been to emphasize the distinctness of God from the world that the naive reaction is to take the image for the reality itself and so think of God as literally out or up there. In fact for all the theistic religions God is omnipresent, and therefore as much present in one area of our space as any other. Thus talk of God's transcendence or immanence (of him being beyond or in the world) turn out to be metaphors, which can easily bewitch us into drawing illegitimate conclusions. Revelation may sometimes be a case of God intervening in the world, but it should certainly not always be understood in this way.

'To reveal' means literally in its Latin roots 'to draw back the veil from'. It is thus a disclosure of what might otherwise have remained hidden from view. Continuing the theme of omnipresence, God is present in everything sustaining it in existence, but it is a presence which we might never have seen had it not been for grace, the kindly disposition of God to man, which means that God is always taking initiatives to draw us closer to himself. These the major religions identify with certain key or paradigmatic events, but it would be a mistake to think of revelation exclusively in these terms; for in addition each of them would wish to suggest that God has so made us that corresponding to our search is God's disclosure of himself in the natural order of the world.

Revelation through the world and its symbols

Take, for instance, experiences of awe and wonder. Many religions would claim that these experiences should not be viewed as mere accidents. They reflect the fact that the Creator has put something of himself into the world he has created. We see it as beautiful because the divine artist has gifted us with something of his own powers of creativity. Likewise each moral challenge is seen as a call to be like him who is perfect goodness. That is why Paul can claim in the opening chapters of his Letter to the Romans that pagans already have the divine moral law written on their hearts. Of course this is not to claim that every moral precept is crystal clear – far from it. But it is to suggest that there is a Love beckoning that leaves most of us dissatisfied with just getting by, just doing the bare minimum, and that this discontent with a purely selfish existence is there for a reason. It is implanted by God to draw ourselves to him and his purposes for us.

Much Protestant theology is deeply suspicious of this sort of approach. The feeling seems to be that it must inevitably detract from the heart of true revelation as contained in the Bible. For, though it can be expressed, as I have done above, in terms of God reaching out to human beings in the way he has made the natural world, it inevitably suggests the ability of us to reach God, for us to take the initiative, since the veil lies at hand for us to lift. That is why in much contemporary Protestant theology contemptuous reference is made to 'religion', all human attempts to seek for God, as distinct from God's disclosure of himself in Christ: Karl Barth, Dietrich Bonhoeffer and Eberhard Jüngel are three obvious twentieth-century examples. The issue is certainly an important one, for on your answer to this question will depend not only your valuation of the Bible and the natural world but also your attitude to other religions, and indeed your general attitude to the culture of which you form part. Such thinkers (of which Luther and Calvin are earlier examples) want to say that the human mind is too blinded by sin to say anything of value until it has been converted to Christ. My own personal belief in the Incarnation is no less firm than theirs, but for that very reason I find their convictions strange. Could a God who involves himself with the world to the degree that is implied in this doctrine really abandon the world in every other respect? It is precisely for that reason that my Christianity demands belief in a God who expresses himself in other religions and also in secular culture, though obviously as a Christian I believe this only reaches its fullest expression in Christ.

Certainly it would be very difficult to substantiate the claim that it has always been Christianity which has been responsible for major advances in society. Indeed, it is not clear to me that Christianity brought as much compassionate concern for others to the societies of which it formed the basis as Islam. For, though it removed from the moral landscape sores like exposure of unwanted infants, almsgiving never occupied as central a place as in Islam, where it forms one of the 'five pillars', thus producing a primitive welfare state long before this was so in Christian countries. Again, although Christianity may have had the corrective available in passages like Galatians 3:28, ('In Christ there is neither male nor female'), in practice the initiative for the equality of women came from secular culture instead. Finally, though I myself am not a vegetarian, those of my readers who are will have to look to eastern religions for precedent, not western.

But even then we have not touched the depths of our debt to 'natural theology', this appeal to God's revelation in the natural order. For the very symbols we use of God in the Bible often come from this shared universal experience of God. Take heaven and sacrifice as two examples. People often speak patronizingly of primitive cultures as though the sky was populated with gods simply because these early societies didn't know any better, but Christians at least ought to be a little more careful, especially when they recall that the Lord's Prayer itself opens with the invocation 'Our Father who art in Heaven', and heaven is just another word for the sky. In fact the Greek word for God and the name of its principal god, Zeus, are both derived from a word in the parent language that means 'sky' – but that is not to say that the early Greeks thought that the sky was god, or even that the gods necessarily lived there. In much poetry the mountain of Olympus is the favoured candidate, while in more reflective thinking the gods are denied physical existence at all. Rather, the point is that the sky or the heavens are seen as particularly revelatory of the nature of God, as a vehicle through which God symbolizes what he is truly like – vast, without limit, incapable of being fully comprehended by us, but also at the same time essentially trustworthy (think of the regularity of the appearance of sun and moon) and gracious (both Jesus and Paul in Acts refer to the beneficence of God in sending the rain – Matthew 5:45 and Acts 14:17). There are quite a number of factors which explain why we do not immediately think in the same way, one obvious one being that most of us now live in towns. Poets can sometimes help us to recapture the mood, as in Gerald Manley Hopkins's poem beginning 'The world is charged with the grandeur of God'. But, whether that is so or not, what I am concerned to stress is the extent to which religious symbolism draws from revelation in the natural order, and the perils that ensue if these symbols are interpreted too literally. John Robinson's *Honest to God* was a best-seller in the 1960s. Part of his concern was to replace the God 'up there' with the God at the deepest level of our being. But a major defect of his book was his failure to stress that both are equally just metaphors and that both are therefore compatible with one another, with one image more appropriate in some circumstances rather than others. Thus one does not worship one's deepest self, but that which is infinitely above one and the gracious source of one's existence.

Sacrifice is another feature of primitive religion that is easily misunderstood. It can be, and no doubt often was, seen simply as a form of barter. One gave the gods something of worth in the hope of gaining something of worth in return, or at least of keeping them on one's side. This is no worse than the attitude of some present-day believers to prayer and church-going. But there was something deeper at stake in the practice and it is as well to be aware of what this is, as Judaism, Christianity and Hinduism have all evolved out of earlier sacrificial practices. Two fundamental acknowledgements seem to have been intended by such rites. First, everything belongs to God as its source and so in recognition of this fact one gives something back in gratitude. Ancient Israel had its burnt offerings and also the sprinkling of the blood on the altar – a messy business, but symbolizing that the very life-blood coursing through our veins comes as a gift from God; Hinduism in the early Vedic period had its fire sacrifices. The idea continues in Hindu temples of today with the offering of the *puja*, a very simple offering including the basic constituent of the Indian diet, rice; and similarly in the communion service of many churches today the bread and wine are first offered with the words: 'Blessed are you, Lord God of all creation. Through your goodness we have this bread to offer, which earth has given and human hands have made.' The second major acknowledgement is that no reconciliation, no restoration of a broken relation, can occur without cost. That was why a valuable animal was given to God, not just any creature from the flock or herd. Of course, the danger in all symbols is that the symbol will be taken to exhaust the reality, and so nothing further need be done. It was for this reason that several of the Hebrew prophets inveighed against the practice. But it was eventually to provide a model or analogy for understanding Jesus's own death, though again sometimes with the corresponding difficulty of people thinking that with the sacrifice made nothing further needs to be done on their part. Sacrifice is thus another example of a natural symbol which was to play a major role in revealed religion. Experience of the world as 'graced' and beneficially ordered led inevitably to certain practices which were then to run deeply into the character of revealed religion as well, which would once more seem to argue against any very sharp demarcation line between where the revelation implicit in natural religion ends and that in revealed theology begins.

Revelation through texts

But what are we to understand by revelation proper? We have already rejected the suggestion that it has anything to do with visitors from outer space. But that does not mean that we must therefore go to the opposite extreme, and think in terms of a purely human product. One of the sad things about contemporary theology is the tendency to extremes, to suppose on the one hand that the only way of defending revelation is to think of the Bible as coming literally from the hand of God as in fundamentalism, or on the other to suppose that because the human contribution is at times all too evident it must all be explained in this way. This is as silly as thinking that because so much of what I think and do can be explained by factors outside my control, there is no need to speak of a distinct contribution from myself, for example in my thinking or in my dialogue with others. A lot of the problems seem to be generated by a false dichotomy, by the supposition that the only alternative to a natural explanation is a miraculous one, that if God interacts with his world this can only be in terms of violation of various natural laws or laws of science. But, if one thinks for a moment about our own interaction with each other, there are no physical, psychological or sociological laws which could, even in principle, offer a *complete* explanation of the way people think. This is what it means to accept that human beings have free will. But, if that is so, all the religious believer is doing in asserting his belief in revelation is acknowledging a potential additional dialogue partner, in the workings of God upon our unconscious or sometimes more explicitly in visions or auditions, where miracle would be involved. It is interesting, however, to observe how seldom this latter type of claim is made in the Bible.

Admittedly the Bible is often spoken of as 'God's word' and in modern liturgies the reader is often urged to say at the end, 'This is the word of the Lord.' Similarly in Judaism in traditional synagogue worship the Torah is treated with enormous respect. Still written on a scroll, it is ceremoniously removed from its special cupboard (called the Ark) and then read by the reader, who follows the words not with his finger but with a pointer, specially made for the purpose and usually of silver. Likewise the Quran is treated by Muslims with great respect. They will always wash carefully before touching the book and the traditional stress on Muhammad's illiteracy only serves to stress the extent to which it is peculiarly God's word.

But it is important in all of this not to lose sight of why the words are being accorded such value. For though the text has often in all religious traditions been read in a very literal-minded way, it is not the words themselves that have ever been held to be of value, but rather their power to communicate to the person listening. In short, they are seen as revelatory, as disclosing God, and that is what makes them of value, although inevitably not all that is said has the same power to disclose the nature and purposes of God. So in describing a particular text as revelatory, one is saying that it has a peculiar power for disclosing the divine, rather than claiming that chapter and verse will self-evidently be perceived as the detailed, specific and literal words of God. In fact, as we shall see, different aspects of a revelatory text have assumed prominence at different historical periods. A good example of this from within Hinduism is the status of the early *Vedas*. These are the most ancient, sacred texts of Hinduism, and the word *veda* actually means revelation – 'knowledge given by God'. Nevertheless in the practice of Hinduism they have declined in importance whilst the later *Upanishads* have assumed central significance and the still later *Bhagavadgita* is not far behind.

However, one should not necessarily think of this as always a progressive phenomenon. A good example of the power of a neglected text to come alive as revelatory once more would be recent attitudes to the role of the Old Testament and the key role it has exercised in shaping Liberation theology's concern for social justice (to be discussed in chapter 4). Or there is the Reformation's perspective of itself as rediscovering a forgotten Paul with his stress on justification by faith. In the Introduction I stressed how important it is to be aware of the way in which all sacred texts are read in the context of a community of tradition that assigns relative and changing values to the material. But it is just as important to take account of the fact that the very existence of the sacred text ensures the possibility of new stresses and perspectives emerging from out of the text to shape subsequent developments of the tradition. Thus in thinking of the role of scripture we need to recognize at least two creative dialogues taking place. There is the original one that has led to the existence of the text in the first place, and then there is the dialogue that continues within the community between existing traditions of interpretation and possible new challenges emerging from the text itself. In the next chapter we shall look at some of the ways in which detailed study of a sacred text can help produce some of these challenges.

Sociology applied to Buddhism and Islam

All my stress so far on the way in which religions operate within a shared community tradition inevitably raises the question of how the role of social factors in its formation is to be assessed. So let us look briefly at the relevance of sociology to the study of religion, as well as at the possibilities of comparing different religious traditions. As examples of the application of sociology to religion I shall take the history of Buddhism and Islam, not because similar points cannot be made about the development of Christianity but simply because later chapters will in any case consider that particular religion in greater detail. They are in any case good examples to take, not only because they had their origins in very different parts of the world (India and Arabia), but also because they date from very different historical periods: Buddhism began in the sixth century BC, while Islam dates from the seventh century AD.

One way of understanding Buddhism is as a protest

movement against the Vedic form of Hinduism, in particular its rigorous class system. The religious backing to this caste system is perhaps seen most clearly in one of the Vedic hymns, the 'Hymn of the Cosmic Man' (X,90), in which this ordering of society is seen as having some sort of cosmic justification, and of course it did at least bring stability to society with everyone knowing their appropriate role and contribution. Buddha lived during a period of change in India when urbanization was taking place, and he had the advantage of viewing the resultant crisis with the dispassionate eye of an outsider, as he appears to have been born in an area un-influenced by or at any rate on the fringes, of Hindu culture, in Bihar on the borders between India and Nepal. There is some evidence to suggest that his earliest followers came from city householders, and that might well be explained in terms of their new-found wealth giving them greater choice over their own destiny. The Buddha's challenge to personal responsibil-ity perhaps produced an answering chord in them, which viewing the present order of society as a divinely determined reality no longer succeeded in doing. For one key difference between Buddha's teaching and early Hinduism is the way in which he replaced the latter's stress on right action, the ritual performance of social duty, with an emphasis on personal responsibility. The primary moral concern has become one of right intention. In this respect it is possible to see some sort of parallel with the Reformation in sixteenth-century Europe: for it was preceded by the Renaissance which certainly laid greater stress on the individual than medieval society had done, and so it at least prepared the ground for Protestantism with its stress on *personal* responsiblity for belief rather than passive accept-ance of the given communal framework. In no way is this supposed to cast doubt on any of these variants of religion. Rather, it merely helps explain the success of the religion at that particular time. In much the same way one can investigate the success of political parties, the rise of Fascism in pre-war Germany or the return to democracy in some Latin-American countries. We can give a sociological explanation of these things without undermining the rightness or wrongness of the claims of either Fascism or democracy.

34

Social factors can also be used to explain how in the later history of Buddhism a much more 'Hindu' or social and ritualistic version of Buddhism emerged within the Mahayana or mainstream northern Buddhist tradition. As already noted, one of the main attractions of the original message of the Buddha had been its strong, individualistic emphasis. But centuries later that came to be seen as one of its main drawbacks. The great mass of the people felt excluded by the claim that it was only possible to pursue enlightenment by becoming a member of the Buddhist community of monks, the *Sangha* and so there developed a more communitarian vision of the religion in which interdependence was stressed.

However, the earlier Theravada tradition still survives in southern Asia, with roughly the same number of adherents as the later, northern Mahayana tradition. But it too, especially in more recent history, has been subject to change brought about by social factors. A still more rationalist and individualistic version of Theravada has emerged, partly in response to Protestant missionaries and partly because of the rise of an educated middle class. No longer content to see the major role assigned to the *Sangha*, they want to claim greater responsiblity for themselves. Thus many would now see it as possible for the layman himself to obtain *nirvana*, final release from the world of striving and desire, without necessarily having to enter the *Sangha* to do so, as more traditional Theravadan beliefs presupposed. Paradoxically, among the poorer classes the move to the cities has often produced a reaction in the opposite direction. Hinduism's offer of patron deities who might look after you in a world of increasing insecurity can often produce a better response than the original Buddhism of their native village.

Though it would be incorrect to say that the divine plays no role in Buddhism (in Theravada the gods are held to exist but not to play any significant role in the world, while in Mahayana cosmic buddhas are appealed to for grace in living one's life), it is certainly at the opposite end of the spectrum to Islam. For Islam the divine initiative absolutely determines its inaugural revelation. Indeed, no religion places a higher regard upon its sacred text. Nor is it hard to see why this should be so.

Tradition has it that the illiterate Muhammad, meditating alone at night in the Hira caves, was greeted by the angel Gabriel who communicated directly to Muhammad the very words of Allah. Also, unlike the earliest version of the Buddhist scriptures, the Pali canon which dates from four to five centuries after the Buddha's death, Muhammad's immediate followers memorized what he said and an authoritative version of the Quran was already in existence by a mere forty years after Muhammad's first revelatory experience, and only twenty years after his death.

This has produced both a great strength and a great weakness. The strength lies in the fact that it can claim, more than any other religion (including Christianity, as we shall see), to have direct contact with its founding prophet's own words. But this has also produced a great potential weakness, as can be seen in the enormous rise of Islamic fundamentalism in the modern world. For because these are seen as God's direct words to Muhammad and not as reported through others, to depart from the letter of the text can seem suspiciously like departing from Islam itself (which in any case means *submission* to God's will), and so any attempt to adapt the message to changed social circumstances can seem suspiciously like heresy or even apostasy.

Yet social factors have of course helped shape the development of Islam as they have shaped all other belief systems. Certainly, social unrest in Mecca and Medina played their part in Muhammad's eventual success. Thanks to the recent rise of a mercantile class there had been a corresponding decline in the clan system along with a reduction in its strong sense of corporate responsibility. Muhammad's message managed to restore that sense by giving it a deeper religious grounding and thus at the same time once more reinvigorated social cohesion. Yet we must stress that this does not mean that Muhammad's success can be wholly explained in this way. Perhaps largely because Muhammad was a post-Christian phenomenon, there is a long tradition within Christianity of casting doubt upon his credentials, particularly his moral credentials. But these are no worse than those of many a Christian hero (like Calvin, who also was responsible for the death of others and married someone very much younger than himself). Muhammad's behaviour can in fact easily be given a charitable explanation in terms of the circumstances of his time. His persistence against considerable odds, the numerous parallels with his divine call that exist among the Old Testament prophets, and the sincerity of his convictions all serve to reinforce his claims. Thus no account of the rise of Islam would be complete which failed to mention Muhammad's conviction of a divine call as an integral part.

But the subsequent history of Islam is as complicated sociologically as that of any other faith. Sunni is the name of the largest branch of Islam, and it derives its name from the 'traditions' of the prophet which are used to supplement the Quran, in terms of the way in which society is run. In addition to the caliphs, central leaders who gave social guidance and judgement, at a very much later stage powerful local guides also emerged under the influence of the mystical Sufi movement. Even as late as the nineteenth century these local interpreters (saints or marabouts) were the real heart of what the typical Muslim would have understood by his religion. Nor is it hard to understand why. In a rural, illiterate society, where central authority was weak and tribal feuds common, one needed arbitrators of what was to be done, and this is the role these saints performed, at times in a way completely at variance with the Quran. Thus even as late as the turn of the century the French novelist André Gide found an easy acceptance of prostitution and sexual licence by them in Algeria that would be inconceivable there now. What has changed is that on the one hand there is now strong central government, thanks to modern communications, and on the other the move to the towns has brought with it a corresponding rise in literacy. The result is that the natural egalitarianism of Islam has reasserted itself, with every individual once more having direct access to the Quran and its teaching. Indeed, President Gaddafy of Libya in the 1970s and 1980s went one stage further than most in even denying status to tradition, not just to the role of the saints. Nor do sociologists think that such a return to fundamentalism is necessarily at all incompatible with adaptation to the modern world. Indeed, it has certain positive advantages. Prayer required five times a day and abstinence for a whole month during Ramadan cannot but help towards a disciplined and therefore hard-working form of existence, while Islam's strong emphasis on alms-giving and egalitarianism are both pressures that work towards social cohesion. One example of the seriousness of intent in Muslim societies to produce their own version of economics compatible with the Quran has been the introduction of interest-free banking to accord with the traditional ban on usury, and the imposition of an alms-tax on all savings.

Because Islam very quickly became the official religion of a state (under the Umayyad dynasty), Sunnis have never really experienced any difficulty in accepting decisions of the state as part of the process whereby their religion is made a reality. The main minority branch of Islam, the Shi'ites, however, has always had a less respectful attitude to state authority. Not only do they dispute the early succession of caliphs, but also one whom they do recognize fell a martyr to Umayyad government troops. There is also a stronger apocalyptic stress, which inevitably relativizes all present social structures, since the belief is that the final twelfth imam (leader) will come to inaugurate the Last Day. It is this branch which has the ascendancy in Iran, which makes comprehensible both the overthrow of the Shah in 1979 and the fervour with which Ayatollah Khomeini's injunctions were followed in the subsequent Iran/Iraq war. The imams, beginning with the first Ali (Shi'ite means 'the party of Ali'), were held to be infallible and so the Sunni appeal to tradition and consensus could be dispensed with. The ayatollahs are thus only temporarily corporately charged with the task of leadership, and this very fact enables one to see how easily any leadership in Iran could be rejected without rejecting the faith as such. The leader would be seen as having failed in his stewardship and it would be his leadership that was at fault, not Islam as such.

Comparing the religions

In looking at the response of some of the major world religions to their sacred texts a number of things should now be clear.

First, not all texts are treated with equal respect. Contrast the attitudes of Hindus to the *Vedas* with that of Muslims to the Quran. For the former, the *Vedas* have now lost much of their authority, whereas of all religions Islam remains most respectful to its sacred text. Secondly, all texts are approached within a communal framework of tradition. Sometimes this is very explicit, as in Islam with its majority group being known as 'the people of the tradition' (Sunni), or in Judaism with the way in which Hebrew even has a special word for the reception of tradition (*kabbalah*). But in all cases it would be a fundamental mistake to expect to be able to read the texts as an uninitiated reader and derive the same insights as the believer. Their meaning within the religion is that given to them by a particular tradition of interpretation, and to sit down and read the sacred texts of another religion without guidance is to open oneself to fundamental distortions, as fundamental as if one attempted to do the same thing with the Christian Bible.

Thirdly, all religions are complex, taking many different forms. Though obviously there are shared characteristics that make them one religion, there are always several streams running parallel within each religion, often with very major differences between them. Thus in Hinduism not only is there great variety in devotion to particular deities, but there is also dispute about how precisely Brahman should be interpreted. The ninth-century thinker, Shankara, advocated a monistic interpretation of the sacred texts, according to which no ultimate distinction should be drawn between the divine Brahman and the human *atman* (soul). Both are part of a single reality, and at death one dissolves back into Brahman. By contrast the eleventh-century philosopher, Ramanuja, adopted a position more like the theistic religions of the West. He held that Brahman, the world and the soul are all separate realities, with the latter two dependent for their existence on the first. Likewise there is the division between Theravada and Mahayana in Buddhism, between Sunni and Shia in Islam, and between Orthodox and Reform in Judaism, not to mention the divisions within Christianity. This is important to note because it indicates the *variety* of responses that have existed within each religion in the past, as well as alerting us to the danger of too easily crediting any one particular position to a religion today.

Again, the capacity of religion to respond to different social conditions is well illustrated by the enormous changes that have sometimes occurred. Witness, for example, the disappearance of sacrificial rites from both Hinduism and Judaism despite their one-time centrality to both. Major changes occur as religions attempt to respond to the modern world. The *bhakti* movement now plays a major role in Hinduism, fundamentalism grows vigorously in Islam, and in Buddhism lay movements are attempting to displace the centrality of the *Sangha*. In Judaism and Christianity there are even attempts to retain the traditions but remove any belief in the objective existence of God – examples of this last-mentioned trend being the American Mordecai Kaplan (d. 1983) within Judaism and the British Don Cupitt (b. 1934) within Christianity.

But if this sheer resourcefulness and adaptability of religion within the apparent constraints of a sacred text constitutes one of the fascinations of comparative religion, another must surely be the shared features. Part of this uniformity can undoubtedly be explained by the natural religion discussed earlier. The same natural symbols suggest themselves. Even the sexual symbolism of Hinduism is not a complete exception: St John of the Cross's mystical poetry is replete with sexual imagery. But what is particularly interesting is the way in which particular tendencies apparently foreign to a given religious tradition seem eventually to find expression. Thus a religion like Christianity which claims that God has been given definitive expression in the Incarnation none the less has found room for a *via negativa* (speaking of God only in terms of what he is not) that corresponds closely to the tradition of *Brahman nirguna*, the 'God without attributes' of the Hindu tradition, just as it has even found room for monistic forms of mystical experience like those of Meister Eckhart (d. 1327). Similarly, religions like Judasim and Islam which are very practical and down-to-earth in their original expression have eventually found room for very mystical variants as with the Kabbalah and Hasidism in Judaism and Sufism in Islam. It is almost as though certain religious emphases have to come to expression eventually, whatever the dominant strain in the tradition.

But though it is possible to detect the hand of God in all of this there is no use pretending that fundamental differences do not remain. There is no easy way of reconciling Judaism to Christianity's belief in Jesus as the Messiah, far less in him as God Incarnate. Again, the Quran claims that Jesus merely swooned on the Cross, though it does accept the Virgin Birth, while Hinduism and Buddhism both find his cry of dereliction from the Cross a sign of weakness, taking this world of pain more seriously than a holy man ought. Some, like the philosopher John Hick, in *God and the Universe of Faiths* (1973), respond to such conflicts by suggesting that a 'Copernican' revolution is required: no longer must we place our own religion at the centre; instead God must be there, with all religions equally distant from him. But this is too easy a solution. We do not think that in any other area of human knowledge everyone has progressed equally. So why should we in this? But equally there is no need to return to the position of assuming truth to lie exclusively only in one. Instead, we need to see all as containing various mixtures of truth and falsehood. Of course, this could easily be used as a recommendation for standing outside them all. But only God can do that. We have not the omniscience to judge them all from a totally neutral perspective. Whether one be believer or non-believer one is always coming from somewhere, with certain assumptions and prejudices. So, as is being increasingly recognized in comparative religion, the most one can do is to use such study to allow ones' existing perspective to be challenged as one tries to enter sympathetically into a framework different from one's own system of belief. In the process as a Christian one may be challenged to rediscover the sacredness of the ordinary that is so pervasive in Hinduism or the strong sense of mutual interdependence that is so prominent a feature of Islamic society and allow this to affect one's understanding of Christianity. It may be that all that will be possible may be sympathetic understanding without agreement, as perhaps with fundamentalism in Islam or Jewish nationalism as a response to the Holocaust; but even where

agreement is not reached, understanding is surely worth while. For even that which on first sight may appear contemptible can become perceived as a part of a framework of what is religiously right and good, as in the caste system's attempt to secure a stable society or the use of very explicit sexual symbolism like the *lingam* (black stone phallus to represent Shiva) as a means of identifying the divine as the source of all creativity. Both these examples are from Hinduism and illustrate well how what initially appears simply to be very primitive practice can through detailed study come to be seen as having its own inherent rationality and intelligibility.

In the next chapter I shall pursue this question of the mixture of truth and falsehood in revealed religion by examining more closely the specific case of Christianity and the way in which it has had to come to terms with a more complex view of its own sacred texts.

2

The Bible's Theologians

History or theology?

In the previous chapter one of my principal concerns was to ensure that the reader did not misunderstand the nature of myth and thus human beings' earliest attempts at theology. Far from being primitive attempts at science, they are in the main to be understood as part of the human search for meaning. They provide an intelligible framework to live by, but their use is governed by very different rules from those that pertain once society moves to completely conceptual or abstract ways of thinking. I also mentioned in passing that the Bible, though essentially post-mythological, none the less retains many transitional characteristics. Whether that is agreed or not, what is of vital importance is to acknowledge that its world is very different from our own and that, just as myth will be totally misunderstood unless one is aware of the different rules of thinking in operation, so exactly the same applies in the case of the Bible. Indeed, in some ways the danger of projecting our own world on to that of the Bible is greater than in the case of myth – for everyone is surely aware that scientific explanation only really became a concern in the modern world, whereas very few people seem to be aware of how different was the attitude to history in the ancient world compared to our own. Leopold von Ranke, the German nineteenth-century historian who is commonly regarded as the founder of modern scientific history, in a famous phrase described the task of the historian as simply to record 'how it really was' (*wie es eigentlich gewesen*); but no ancient writer would have agreed. Instead there was

43

always some further purpose in view, to which the mere recording of events was subordinate. This meant that there was often what would seem to us a rather cavalier attitude to the 'facts', but before we rush in to pronounce it so, we need to become aware of the very different assumptions that were operating within that society. In the Bible's case the history was always subordinate to theological purpose, and that is why I have entitled this chapter 'The Bible's Theologians'. Throughout what follows I shall try to indicate what the different assumptions were, so that we shall be better able to assess the biblical writers in terms of what they themselves were attempting to achieve, rather than what we anachronistically impose on them.

Trying to understand this different world with its different rules is for me one of the fascinations of studying the Bible. But there are of course many others. Critical study of the Bible is, like history itself, a relatively young discipline; both were only effectively launched in the nineteenth century. Since then probably no other text has been investigated in anything like the same degree of detail. Every possible technique seems to have been used to get at both the books' constitutive elements and the reasons behind their present shape. The techniques known as source, form and redaction criticism (all explained here later) have all been tried, as well as meticulous comparative work on the literature, history and archaeology of the surrounding culture. In what follows I shall try to illustrate the relevance of some of these methods. The very speed of developments in this area constitutes one of its attractions, for the student cannot help but be aware that this is a subject where much still remains be to resolved, though new discoveries like the Dead Sea Scrolls in 1947 or new methods like redaction criticism, first proposed in the 1950s, are continually advancing increased possibilities for understanding.

Yet it cannot be denied that many a believing Christian has found the whole approach profoundly disconcerting. He or she has hitherto taken the Bible simply as a straightforward historical record of God's dealings with humanity, whereas now they are presented with something immeasurably more complex. Unfortunately at this point biblical scholars are seldom of much help. So concerned are they to play the role of the scientific historian that they forget that not only are contemporary secular historians generally less confident than Ranke was about the total objectivity of history (I shall have more to say about this in chapter 3), but that even after all this valuable spade-work is done, the basic question remains. The biblical writers have used history as a medium to speak about God, and the question that remains is whether we can continue to endorse their own verdict on themselves: that God speaks through them. For this reason I shall end this chapter by offering a way of understanding God's involvement in that complex process.

OLD TESTAMENT SURPRISES

Moses' enlarged role

Traditionally the first five books of the Bible were ascribed to the authorship of Moses, but ever since the latter half of the nineteenth century and the application of source criticism to the documents this has looked increasingly unlikely. However, not only has his role here been called into question but also whether the actual narrative within the books reflects his real historical role or rather a considerably enlarged and 'fictitious' version of it. But that very label 'fictitious' indicates the considerable problems involved in making a fair assessment across more than two thousand years. To us, of course, to present anyone other than he actually was is to tell a culpable untruth. But that is not, as we shall see, how the ancient mind worked. Indeed, for me the more interesting question is this: what was it that produced the desire to attribute so much to Moses? But first let me illustrate how source criticism has come to the conclusions it has.

In chapter 1 we have already noted the way in which inconsistencies between the two versions of the creation myth in the opening chapters of Genesis provide some reason for postulating different sources. Were this the only case of a doublet (two versions of the same incident), the elaborate theory of four sources for the Pentateuch would never have been postulated. But similar problems emerge, for instance in the story of the Flood, with Noah being told in one place to take one pair of each kind of animal into the Ark and in another seven (contrast Gen. 6:19 and 7:2), while there are equally conflicting accounts of its duration, from a year and ten days (Gen. 7:11) to forty days plus three periods of seven days (Gen. 7:4 and 8:6). Again, Exodus 6 speaks of God's name being revealed as Yahweh for the first time, while in Genesis 4 it is assumed that the name has been in use from very early times. Again Deuteronomy, unlike Exodus 20:24, assumes that sacrificial worship is going to be confined to one place and that only Levites may be priests (contrast Exod. 28:1).

It is of course only possible to present the theory in barest outline here, and a whole range of considerations would have to be taken into account in considering the argument in detail. But in outline two early sources, J and E, have been identified, so named because one of their distinguishing features is the different names they use for God. 'J' speaks of Jehovah, or more accurately *Yahweh*. (Jehovah is in fact a corruption of the name, created by scribes to avoid using this most holy name for God. The consonants in Yahweh were combined with the vowels in Adonai, Lord.) The slightly later 'E' source, on the other hand, used *Elohim*, which is actually the plural Hebrew word for 'gods'. E thus reflects Israel's growth into monotheism out of an original polytheism, though at this stage no polytheism was intended by its use of the word. The 'D' source we know to be a much later development still, because sacrifice in more than one place is accepted even by devout Israelities like Samuel and Elijah as the norm in the time of the early monarchy, several hundred years after the events to which Deuteronomy alledgedly refers, and it is for this reason that the writing of D is often associated with a reform in the cult under King Josiah in 621 that centralized all worship in Jerusalem. Finally, 'P' does not even find it necessary to command such a centralization. He simply assumes it, and for this reason is thought to be later still, especially as he narrows the priesthood still further to the house of Aaron, just as Ezekiel, writing in the sixth century, attempts to do so by limiting it to the family of Zadok.

To the modern mind the most difficult aspect to accept is undoubtedly the idea of so much being attributed to Moses when none of it comes from his own hand. This is a problem by no means unique to the Pentateuch. Some of the prophets have material included that belongs to a later age. For instance, modern scholars distinguish Second Isaiah (chs 40–55) as well as Third Isaiah (ch. 56–66), while almost certainly at least two gospels attributed to original disciples, Matthew and John, do not actually come from their own hands. In the twentieth century to make such attributions smacks of deceit, whereas the ancient mind thought very differently. Our own culture is one which places a high premium on notions like progress, innovation, change and youth. But one must remember that before the rise of science the notion of progress was by no means nearly so obviously a good, and that not only in the myth of the Garden of Eden but in ancient society generally change was viewed with suspicion. Thus Greek legend too had its myth of the Golden Age (under the god Kronos) and it was the judgement of the elders which was sought in legal disputes (the word for 'elder' in Greek, *presbyteros*, was by contraction to produce our word for priest). It was little wonder, then, that in attempting to justify change models and precedents were sought in the past, and the argument was conducted in terms of what Moses would have legislated for today, had he faced current circumstances, just as the authors of the first and fourth gospels presumably conceived of themselves as writing what Matthew and John would have written had they lived long enough. Nor is the phenomenon by any means confined to the Jewish world.

Parallel examples of laws being credited to shadowy founders of Greek cities can also be found. Indeed, even today occasional instances can be found. The Methodist peer Lord Soper, speaking on the 250th anniversary of Wesley's conversion in 1988, claimed that Wesley would have been a socialist had he been living today, despite the fact that he had in actual life been a High Tory. Today we tend to try to legitimize our claims to truth by reference to 'science'; in those days they legitimized their claims by reference to the great men of the past.

The question has even been raised whether the central traditions of Exodus and Sinai did not perform a very much smaller role than that which our text now accords them. For instance, in the 1950s the biblical scholar Gerhard von Rad, reflecting on the creed of Deuteronomy 26:5–9, asked whether, since it makes no reference to Sinai, the Exodus and Sinai might not once have constituted entirely separate traditions. In other words, they once constituted the experience of two entirely different groups of people. More recently Norman Gottwald in his *Tribes of Yahweh* (1979) has carried the doubts further. His suggestion is that a minority returning from Egypt gave to the local rural population their own ideology of a liberator God. This then gave these countryside dwellers the necessary inspiration to take over from the more developed city-state dwellers who also inhabited the land. Such theories are all much more speculative than the source hypothesis, but I mention them for two reasons: first, they illustrate well how open many issues remain, and secondly because it cannot too strongly be stressed how different the biblical attitude to history was from our own.

The essential point can be put in terms of the contrast between a search for meaning and a search for history. However small-scale Moses' success in fact had been, it was taken as the true measure of the way things should be. The later history of Israel can furnish examples of the same process in reverse. We know from contemporary secular inscriptions that Omri was Israel's greatest king since Solomon, but the world's estimate was not the religious estimate of the author of the Book of Kings, and he is relegated to the insignificance of a couple of sentences (I Kings 16:23–8). Likewise Sepphoris was in fact the capital of Galilee until it was succeeded in AD 18 by Tiberias, and it was only a mere three miles distant from Nazareth; but because it played no role in the life of Jesus, despite its secular importance it is not mentioned once in the Gospels.

But it is vital that neither of two false conclusions should be drawn from what we have said so far. First, just because many facts about Moses have been called into question, it does not follow that all are therefore equally without credence.

Secondly, just because the rules about what might legitimately be attributed to a past historical figure are different from our own, it does not by any means follow that anything goes.

Thus, on the first point, despite the extent of what has been called into question about our knowledge of Moses, we can still be confident both that Moses existed and that his historical role was decisive in securing the liberation of a significant proportion of the population from Egypt. Indeed, many of the more radical theories often involve highly contentious reading of the evidence. So, for example, Gottwald interprets 'inhabitants of the land' to refer to their rulers or kings – and despotic ones at that. The fact that we are dealing with such an early period of history of course means that a dearth of external corroborating evidence is inevitable. Such knowledge as we do have of Egypt and Caanan at the time does on the whole accord well with the biblical account. Yet there are some conspicuous exceptions, such as the fall of Jericho, where archaeological evidence has yielded so far only unsuitable dates. But the existence of the Hyksos dynasty in Egypt and their patronage of other foreigners fits easily with Joseph's stay in Egypt. The reference to the Israelites as slaves building Pithom and Raamses (Exod. 1:11) finds confirmation in the fact that under Raameses II, Raamses was built on the site of Avaris, the former Hyksos capital, while we know that he also carried out building work at Pithom. Indeed the connection of Moses with Egypt may even find confirmation in his very name, since it is a common component in Egyptian names like Thutmose or Ahmose.

If the Exodus took place under Rameses II this would date it to the thirteenth century BC, a full three centuries before the earliest of our four sources, J, which is commonly dated to the reign of Solomon (961–922). This of course would give plenty of time for errors to develop in the tradition. But at the same time one should not exaggerate this. Non-literate peoples have an amazing capacity to remember vast amounts by heart, an ability which in the West we have almost wholly lost. Even today some Muslim tribesmen are able to remember accurately the entire Quran. Poetic passages are easier to commit accurately to memory and so we can be confident that those short passages in the Pentateuch that are in poetry are much more likely to take us closer to the events themselves. Indeed, some scholars suggest that the Song of Miriam (Exod. 15:21) could well be contemporaneous with the actual crossing of the Red Sea.

However that may be, changes did undoubtedly occur, but it would be a mistake to infer that because to our mind they are often very large they were therefore entirely arbitrary, bearing no relation to what was seen as the original revelation to Moses. In fact, all four sources are united in their conviction that what happened to Moses must be seen as definitive or paradigmatic for understanding their own age's standing in relation to God. All use the theme of 'covenant' to express this, that God has entered into a special relationship with Israel in liberating their ancestors from oppression in Egypt. Where they differ is in the different stress they feel is necessary if that relationship is to continue to be a reality in their own times. Thus J, writing at the time of the nation's greatest prosperity under Solomon, finds his most natural response in celebration and gratitude for this intimacy, whereas E, writing a hundred or more years later with the nation now divided into two small separate kingdoms of Israel (in the north) and Judah (in the south), realizes that the main challenge to be faced is the danger of assimilation to the pagan practices of their large neighbours. Accordingly, to counteract that threat, all the anthropomorphisms that had been popular in the time of J are eliminated from his version of events. So for example J's charming image of God walking in the garden of Eden in the cool of the day (Gen. 3:8) could never have been tolerated by E because of its openness to an over-literalistic mis-understanding. Again, D is writing at a time of hope for religious revival in the southern kingdom, and attempts to reinforce this by envisaging Moses as insisting that the covenant needs to be renewed afresh in each generation (cf, for examples, Deut. 6:20–25). Finally, P performs his task at a time when both nations have fallen subject to foreign domination, and his antidote for this is to suggest that the only way of ensuring the continuance of national identity is by careful observance of all the traditions of past, ritual as much as ethical; hence the strange mixture of both in the book of

Leviticus. Nor have these attempts to apply the experience of Moses to one's own day ceased with these four authors. As we shall see in chapter 4, this is precisely what Liberation theology is attempting to do in the present-day circumstances of Latin America.

Obviously this is not the place to pursue in detail the nature of the changes made. But one example may suffice to illustrate the way in which they remained changes within controlled limits. The version of the Ten Commandments with which one is likely to be familiar comes from P (Exod. 20:1–21), but we also have versions from J (Exod. 34:10–28), from E (Exod. 21:22–23:19), and from D (Deut. 5:1–22). Some are closer than others, but all have the prohibition of other gods, of graven images, and of work on the sabbath. So far as the last is concerned, J gives no reason, E one of compassion ('so that your ox and your donkey may rest and the son of your slave girl have a breathing space, and the stranger too'–Exod. 23:12), while D reminds Israel that they too were once slaves; whereas P refers back to his creation narrative with God resting on the seventh day. This last is in fact only in apparent rather than real conflict with the others, for P shows himself elsewhere fully aware of considerations of compassion. Rather, P's reason is an attempt to deepen the compassionate motive by suggesting that such need for rest is built into the very nature of things by God himself. Nor should we think of such freedom with the original as ending with the Bible itself: for even today, although all churches use P's version, Roman Catholics and Lutherans, unlike other denominations, combine other gods and graven images into a single commandment and subdivide coveting neighbour's house and neighbour's wife into two commandments, presumably for precisely the same reasons that led D to place coveting one's neighbour's wife first (contrast Exod. 20:17 and Deut. 5:21). Otherwise, there was the danger of inferring that women should be seen simply as a form of property.

Prophets, not predicters

I want to move on now to look briefly at the other major types of Old Testament literature, beginning with prophecy. Here the most important thing is to disabuse oneself of the idea that the primary role of the prophets was ever seen to be that of predicting the future. The term that they would have used of themselves was the Hebrew word *nabi*, which refers either to their 'call' by God or to the fact that it is their task to issue a 'call' or summons to others on his behalf. Our own word is based on the Greek translation, but even in Greek 'prophet' originally meant an interpreter of the divine and only came to mean a predicter because part of that interpretation may of course involve some reference to the future. Thus it is only once we see them in their own terms that we shall properly understand them. Any reference to the future always remains subordinate to their primary intention, which is their desire to address God's call for repentance and justice to their contemporaries.

Indeed, even when a reference to the future was made, it was seldom specific and, as the Old Testament scholar Robert Carroll has pointed out in *When Prophecy Failed* (1979), such allusions were in any case always qualified in two ways. First, in respect of threats of doom repentance was always seen as opening the possibility of non-fulfilment, as a passage like Jeremiah 18:7–10 makes abundantly clear. Secondly, promises could equally always be seen as containing a measure of truth through the 'remnant motif'. For most seem to have envisaged that only a minority would remain loyal to God and so survive to enjoy something of what was promised. The reason why prophecy has none the less so often been misunderstood is partly because the Christian Bible classes Daniel as a prophet. In fact, as we shall see, he belongs to a quite different genre of literature, the apocalyptic. More importantly perhaps, some of the New Testament, particularly Matthew's Gospel, makes numerous claims that specific verses in the Old Testament have now achieved their fulfilment in Christ.

Since this adds to the confusion, it is worth pausing for a moment to consider what Matthew had in mind. Certainly his use of the Old Testament often gives the impression of being very wooden. So, for example, at the beginning of chapter 21 he assumes that Jesus needs both an ass and a colt to fulfil the 'prophecy' of Zechariah 9:9, thus contradicting Mark 11:2, whereas in fact the original is a case of parallelism, a common feature of Hebrew poetry whereby one said the same thing twice in two slightly different ways. In other words, Zechariah had certainly only ever intended to refer to one animal. Again, at 27:9 he muddles up who said what, and attributes to Jeremiah what in fact again comes from Zechariah (11:12). Indeed, on one occasion he even inserts a negative that gives the opposite sense to the original (cf. Mic. 5:2 and Mat. 2:6). Such errors may suggest that he was using an existing collection of proof-texts rather than checking as he wrote. But, whatever his method was, this lack of attention to the sense of the original indicates that he found his justification for such use in something quite other than confidence in specific predictions. Rather, so convinced was he that Jesus was the culmination of the entire general sweep of the Old Testament that probably one verse would have done just as much as any other to underline the point. In other words, the quotations are there to encourage a Christian re-reading of the Old Testament and its meaning, and so their value must stand or fall not with the success of particular predictions but with the Christian revelation as such and its overarching claim about the direction towards which the entire Old Testament was leading in Christ. Against that primary claim the strangeness of his demonstration shades into insignificance.

Once, then, we have jettisoned any notion of prediction constituting a major element in the prophetic role, their real concerns can at last begin to emerge in their proper light. They have a vision of individual and nation responding to the divine covenant in such a way that none is marginalized but all can find their proper place. Hence a recurring theme is the call for social justice, particularly for those least able to care for themselves – 'the stranger, the fatherless and the widow' (e.g. Jer. 7:6). That the message of the prophets cannot be narrowly confined to purely individualistic notions of salvation is thus one lesson that modern study of the text has forced upon us.

Another is that the traditional Protestant contrast of the prophet of the word standing against the ritualistic priest cannot be allowed to continue, except at any rate in a very modified form. For though of course there are famous passages in the prophets attacking the sacrificial system (e.g. Amos 5:25 or Mic. 6: 6–8), it now appears that there was a much closer relationship between prophet and priest than was once thought, and so such critiques should probably be seen as emerging from within the system rather than in opposition to it. The fact that Isaiah had his commissioning vision in the Temple (Isa. 6:1) and that Ezekiel was himself a priest (Ezek. 1:3) should in any case have given pause for thought. But Sigmund Mowinckel for one, in his *The Psalms in Israel's Worship* (1962), has strengthened the case by demonstrating the cultic role of the Psalms and the effect these have had in turn on the prophets' writings. So, for example, Habakkuk is thought to be directly modelled on the Psalms, with his first two chapters now being interpreted as a cultic lament expressive of the people's distress and appealing to God for help, and his third and last chapter providing assurance of that help.

Apocalyptic dreams

As I mentioned earlier, one reason for misunderstanding the nature of the prophetic writings has been the fact that in our English Bibles Daniel is classed as one of the prophets, whereas in the original Hebrew Bible he is included among what are called 'the Writings'. This category mistake has led to legions of misinterpretations. There is no doubt that the book is full of predictions. But that still does not mean that the book was ever intended to be read in that light. For the so-called 'predictions' have a quite other role, just as is also the case in the only book-length example of this 'apocalyptic' genre in the New Testament, the Book of Revelation.

The reason why scholars date Daniel to a much later period in Jewish history than the book claims is not because of a lack of belief in the power of prediction but because this later period is the only point at which the author is really accurate about historical events. The book claims to be visions of the future of someone called Daniel writing in the sixth century BC. But the only time it touches earth, as it were, is in chapter 11, where it gives an accurate account of events in the second century BC. Of later events it is inaccurate, such as the predicted death of Antiochus Ephiphanes, the Seleucid King of Syria, which did not take place in Israel as foretold. But so equally is it inaccurate about earlier events to an extraordinary degree. For example, Belshassar is portrayed as the successor of his father, Nebuchadnezzar, though in fact he was the son of Nabonid and never reigned as king. Again, the story of Nebuchadnezzar turning into a beast seems to be based on an incident in the life of Nabonid – correctly attributed in the Dead Sea Scrolls. Or, to give a last and glaring example, there never seems to have been a king called 'Darius the Mede' (Dan. 5:31), though there was a famous Darius the Great who ruled over the Persian Empire that succeeded that of the Medes.

In the nineteenth century discoveries such as these did produce something of a crisis. But there is no reason for them to do so today, because we now understand so much better the point of this type of literature. Daniel was written at a time of crisis to encourage the beleaguered faithful. (The Greek ruler of Palestine, Antiochus Ephiphanes, was imposing pagan practices on the country). Precisely by looking at the larger sweep of history the author feels enabled to say that God's purposes will win through in the end, and so casts his confidence into the form of predictions made by an obscure hero from the past. It seems highly unlikely that the author ever really thought of himself as being able to persuade his contemporaries that this book had been lost for four centuries and had only now turned up at exactly the right moment; rather, what he has engaged in is a not too dissimilar exercise from the Pentateuchal sources' treatment of Moses. But, whereas they adapted Moses' teaching to be more relevant to the circumstances of their time, our author here leaves Daniel in the distant past but invites us to take an imaginative journey through time with him up to the author's own day. That way Daniel can use the march of history to inspire confidence, despite the appalling character of present circumstances. In other words, whereas in the one case Moses speaks to the present by being brought into it, in this case Daniel is made to speak by firmly emphasizing his historical distance from that present.

Admittedly the Book of Revelation does not concern itself

with such a wide sweep of history, but if you try to make sense of its predictions, you are going to have just as hard a time of it. For again it is not really the details that matter: its purpose was to help Christians to survive the persecutions of the 90s under Domitian. Of course the Roman Empire did not come to the dramatic end foretold, and indeed lasted several more centuries. Nor have we any more reason to think that the end of the world will take precisely the form predicted. But that by no means makes the book an irrelevance, since its rationale, as with all apocalyptic literature, lies quite elsewhere.

There are two absolutely crucial points that need to be made if we are to understand apocalyptic books like Daniel and Revelation. First, the Bible contains a well-known proverb that 'where there is no vision, the people perish' (Prov. 29:18). To survive in the future we need hope in the present, and that was precisely what these books gave. Though I am not personally sympathetic to Marxism, it surely must be conceded that one of its great strengths is that by offering a vision of a very different world, of universal equality and brotherhood, it has produced unparalleled commitment and resolve for change in the Third World, even in the most adverse of circumstances. In short, apocalyptic literature succeeded in giving the people an alternative vision of the future, precisely at the moment when they most needed it.

Secondly, there is after all a sense in which apocalyptic is fulfilled, though usually in a very different sense from what the author envisaged. God's ultimate purposes do prevail, even if the details of those purposes differ markedly from what was predicted. So, for example, Daniel 7 sees the victory of the Jewish saints symbolized by a heavenly Son of Man. That figure reappears in the New Testament, and though Daniel clearly meant it to refer to his own times, Christians are entitled to see it symbolically fulfilled in the Risen Christ including and drawing all people to himself as the person God intended us all to be. Again, the vision of the woman and the dragon in Revelation 12 reminds us that the Christian's victory has already been symbolically achieved in Jesus, and so victory over all the forces of evil can even be celebrated in the here and now, just as the author of Revelation himself does in chapter

15. To some this may seem like special pleading, but what needs to be recalled is that for the authors themselves, just as much as for any religious believer, God remains firmly in charge and so confidence will always be greater in God's purposes being finally achieved than in them necessarily taking any particular form.

Wisdom's natural theology

In the previous chapter I drew a contrast between revelation through the created order and its symbols and revelation through sacred texts. But classifications are seldom as neat as we would like, and in fact it is increasingly acknowledged that one particular genre of Old Testament literature can best be understood as early attempts at natural theology, as attempts to read the character of God and his purposes for mankind from the natural order. Here one has in mind such books as Proverbs, Eccelesiastes and Job, books that have come to be known as the 'Wisdom literature'. Indeed, in one case we know that the Hebrew writer was so convinced of the value of ordinary human reflection that he has not hesitated to borrow an entire chapter from an Egyptian work, *The Instruction of Amenemopet* (Prov. 22:17–23:11). So ancient Israel seems to have been quite content to tolerate a variety of ways of relating to God, from the sacrificial system, through the inspired utterance of the prophet, to cool reflections of the sage. As one verse puts it: 'Law shall not perish from the priest, nor counsel from the wise, nor the word from the prophet' (Jer. 18:18).

Nor should we attempt too easy a harmonization of all this range of material. For just as today a shared common core conceals a wide variety of views within any particular denomination, so much the same can be said of ancient Israel. For it is not unusual to find authors writing with the specific objective of challenging a received view that has already gained credence within the scriptural canon. Thus the Book of Job is intended to cast doubt on the connection commonly made until then between prosperity and moral goodness, and suffering and evil, as reflected for instance in the Garden of Eden myth (Gen. 3:14–19). Job is portrayed as the wholly righteous man who none the less suffers terribly, and the answer given by God from the whirlwind (ch. 38) is that it is foolish for human beings to expect to understand everything. In a similar way the Books of Jonah and Ruth, possibly written about the same time, were challenging the narrow nationalism of Ezra, who had required Jewish males to divorce their non-Jewish wives (Ezra 9–10). In the former case Jonah is sent to preach to pagan Nineveh, while in the latter David is given a Moabite ancestress in Ruth.

GETTING BEHIND THE GOSPELS

Getting at sources and intentions

No doubt for some readers their interest in investigating the Gospels will be a purely historical one. The challenge will lie in using modern methods to attempt, as it were, to crack the code and discover what sort of historical foundations Christianity has in Jesus, if any. But for many readers this will also be combined with a religious interest, and that will involve at least taking seriously the possibility of Christ having an impact on their own lives. This will mean that for them it is just as interesting to discover what such methods reveal about the nature of the impact of Jesus on the incipient Christian communities. Since this is in many ways the easier of the two questions, I shall postpone saying anything about the historical Jesus himself until we have considerd the nature of the Gospels themselves in some detail.

Source criticism has revealed three main sources of the Gospel tradition (Mark, Q and John), while form and redaction criticism have brought considerable insight into the intentions with which the Gospels were written and earlier traditions modified. I shall therefore now briefly illustrate each in turn.

Even in ancient times it was recognized that a close relation existed between the first three gospels. They see things from a common viewpoint; hence the label 'synoptic' (from the Greek 'seen together'). Augustine explained this in terms of Mark abbreviating Matthew and Luke, but although this theory has had an occasional defender in modern times (for instance, William Farmer), the overwhelming majority of cirtics assume Marcan priority (the view that Mark was written first), although there are in fact eighteen logical possibilities for variants in the relationship between the three.

There are a number of reasons for this. Any notion of a common oral tradition will not do because the parallels are often just too exact, with word for word agreement even down to common asides. For example, Jesus's address to the paralytic is found in *exactly* the same form in all three Gospels (cf. Matt. 9:6; Mark 2:10; and Luke 5:24). Again in their discussion of fasting all three evangelists (Gospel-writers) use the same unusual word for 'wedding-guests'; the Greek literally means 'sons of the bridal chamber' (Matt. 9:15; Mark 2:19; Luke 5:34).

A further reason for postulating that Mark acted as a source for the other two Gospels is that it is easier to explain why Matthew or Luke should want to correct Mark than it is Mark wanting to change the other two. Thus for instance Matthew and Luke omit Mark's reference to Abiathar being high priest when David took bread from God's house, for the very good reason that the priest in question was in fact Ahimelech (Matt. 12:4; Mark 2:26; Luke 6:4 and I Sam. 21:1.) Again, it is easy to understand why Matthew would out of respect for Jesus change Mark 6:5 ('He could do no mighty work there') to Matthew 13:58, ('And he did not do many mighty works there'), or why both Luke and Matthew omit Mark's reference to Jesus being angry in Mark 3:5 (cf. Mark 3:5–6 with Matt. 12:12–14 and Luke 6:10–13). At Mark 10:18 Jesus's 'Why callest thou me good? None is good save even one, God' is re-tained by Luke (18:19), but transformed by Matthew into 'Why askest thou me concerning that which is good?' (Matt. 19:17).

However, lest the reader gain the impression that all changes were motivated out of respect for Christ, let me give one last example that concerns the status of John the Baptist. Luke retains the Marcan image of untying sandals (Mark 1:7, Luke 3:16), whereas Matthew has John say of Jesus: 'He who is coming after me is mightier than I, whose sandals I am not worthy to carry' (Matt. 3:11). Since only non-Jewish slaves were required to untie their master's sandals, the original version gives a very lowly status indeed to John the Baptist, whereas Matthew upgrades him in his desire to make him the first Christian preacher and part of the continuity of Old with New Testament that is, as we have already seen, a recurring theme of his Gospel.

Life would certainly be very much simpler for the student of the New Testament if Mark were the only major source employed by Matthew and Luke. But most scholars accept the existence of a further, anonymous source, called 'Q' (from the German *Quelle*, meaning 'source'). Indeed, even in the passage about John the Baptist to which we have just referred it is commonly thought that Matthew has utilized both sources and modified both. But that is a rather complicated case which we need not go into here. The main reason why scholars think that this further source Q must exist is because we have detailed verbal parallels between Matthew and Luke which are none the less not found in Mark. These parallels are almost exclusively of a teaching rather than narrative kind, and it seems best to explain them by invoking this further source Q which presumably had a special interest in Jesus's teaching.

Two good examples of identical verbal parallels would be Matthew 7:3–5 and Luke 6:41–42 about the speck in one's brother's eye, or Matthew 11:25–27 and Luke 10:21, sometimes known as the 'Johannine thunderbolt' because of its similarity of language about Jesus to John's Gospel. Again, the postulation of a second source would explain why apparently unnecessary doublets occur, as with Matthew giving Jesus's teaching on divorce twice. A clear answer now emerges. One is from Mark (Matt. 19:9) and the other from Q (Matt. 5:32). As for why this should not all be explained by Matthew or Luke borrowing from the other, though this is sometimes canvassed (Michael Goulder is a prominent recent example of a proponent of Luke's dependency on Matthew), the difficulties in the way are pretty overwhelming. If one borrowed from the other, we have to say that they succeded in doing so without betraying any trace of the most characteristic language or theology of the writer from whom they borrowed. Thus if

Matthew borrowed from Luke, why does he not display anything of the beauty of Luke's Greek or his Spirit christology? If the reverse borrowing is proposed, why does the Law nowhere surface as a major theme in Luke? Or why does he not at least borrow those passages unique to Matthew that would reinforce his own picture of Jesus–where Matthew stresses Jesus's compassion (Matt. 8:17) and gentleness (Matt. 12:18–21)?

The simplest explanation is in fact this common independent source Q, with Luke using it more conservatively than Matthew. We have already had some illustrations of Luke's more conservative approach with regard to Mark, and this seems to be repeated with Q. Thus Q is much more organized in Matthew than in Luke, with five major blocks of material. This is perhaps intended to correspond to the five books of the Pentateuch, with Jesus as the new Moses and like Moses finding a mountain as a source of the new law (contrast Matthew's setting of the Sermon on the Mount with Luke 7 and its Sermon on the Plain). Again, if one takes specific verses, it is Matthew who seems more prone to make the changes. To give but two examples, Matthew 23:34 attributes directly to Jesus what Luke 11:49 had ascribed to the Wisdom of God, while the Sermon on the Mount opens with a reference to 'the poor in spirit' in contrast to Luke's 'the poor'.

Such changes of course seem to us an unwarranted freedom with the text. But, as our discussion of the Old Testament should have already amply illustrated, there was a long tradition of very different rules of use and interpretation being held to apply. Just as in that case I stressed that the use of different rules does not necessarily imply a cavalier use of sources, so similarly here one must not draw the implication that Matthew is simply arbitrarily altering his sources to suit his theological purposes. On the contrary, Matthew attributes the saying about the Wisdom of God to Jesus precisely because he believes him to be the divine Wisdom. This he had already demonstrated earlier in his Gospel twice in the space of a single chapter (ch. 11), once in referring to Wisdom by name (v. 19) and once (vv. 28–30) by modelling Jesus's words on the words attributed to Wisdom in the apocryphal book of Eccelesiasticus (cf. ch. 51:23–7). Likewise 'poor in spirit' is not a contradiction of 'poor', a spiritualizing of what had originally a purely material sense; for already in the Old Testament the tradition had begun of using 'poor' of the pious (e.g. Isa. 61:1), and it appears to have this meaning in the Dead Sea Scrolls. In other words, Matthew made the change not to conceal a meaning he did not like, but rather to bring out more clearly a meaning which he thought the expression already had.

This theory of two major written sources (Mark and Q) lying behind the Gospels of Matthew and Luke only dates from 1863 in the works of a German scholar, H. J. Holtzmann, while its impact on England came even later, with B. H. Streeter's writings just before the First World War. But since then, and indeed with increasing frequency since the Second World War, further methods of research have been proposed. There is no need to discuss them all here. All we need note is the way in which Rudolf Bultmann's interest in the inter-war period in form criticism eventually paved the way for the postwar phenomenon of redaction criticism.

Form criticism originally particularly concerned itself with the transmisson of oral traditions about Jesus and the precise form they took prior to their emergence in our present Gospels or in other earlier written documents. In what form were stories about Jesus passed on? How has the life-situation (*Sitz-im-Leben*) of the early church helped shape the precise form in which they have been transmitted? In response to the first question came the answer that much had been preserved in small, separate units, for example as short 'pronouncement stories' with a concluding punch line. Mark 12:13–37, offers four such stories in quick sequence, and one advantage of the theory has in fact been to explain the rather staccato effect of reading this Gospel, as one moves very abruptly from one incident to the next. The reason is that Mark inherited them as separate units with no fixed order for a continuous narrative.

But for me the more interesting question is the second, and the way in which the early church adapted the words of Jesus to ensure that his life and teaching should continue to be a gospel ('good-news') to their own generation. Bultmann was over-confident about the method and seems at times to write as though the only reason for the preservation of a particular saying would be current relevance. But, for example, disputes about sabbath observance do not seem to have been an issue for the post-Resurrection churches, and yet Jesus's disputes on this matter have been recorded in detail. A further problem is that it is often extremely hard to determine whether the 'life-situation' of a particular passage reflects that of the author of the Gospel himself or that of some earlier stage in the transmission of the tradition. In the case of Matthew and Luke we can compare them with each other and with Mark in trying to work out the extent to which the later evangelist has in fact modified an original saying of Jesus to take account of the situation in his own community, but with Mark's Gospel we have no earlier account with which to make comparison. What, for instance, are we to make of Mark 10:12 ('If a woman divorces her husband and marries another, she is guilty of adultery')? These cannot be Jesus's actual words because under Jewish law only husbands had the right to divorce their wives, not wives their husbands, and so there would be no point in Jesus addressing this comment to a purely Jewish audience in Palestine. But under Roman law wives did have such a right. So clearly the verse has been added to an original comment of Jesus about husbands divorcing their wives (Mark 10:11) to show how his teaching can effectively be put into practice in a non-Jewish situation. But did Mark make the alteration, or was it already in his sources? It is hard to tell.

Far easier to resolve is the question of when we may legitimately detect the hand of Matthew or Luke at work in modifying the particular form of something they have inherited from Mark or Q, in order to ensure that Jesus's message continues to speak to their own generation of readers. For instance, if we compare the two versions of the saying of Jesus about the lamp lit in the house in Matthew (5:15) and Luke (11:33), we make the interesting discovery that the former assumes a typical Palestinian one-roomed house, whereas the latter assumes a larger Hellenistic house with a separate entrance passage from which light would shine on those entering it. The former must clearly be Jesus's original words, while in the latter case we find Luke for once treating his sources less conservatively than Matthew, but for the entirely laudable reason of ensuring that the parable would 'come alive' for his Gentile readers.

A more contentious case would be to compare the form of Jesus's reference to a period of tribulation associated with 'the abomination of desolation' in Mark and Luke (Mark 13:14; Luke 21:20). While Mark leaves the reader to work out his own interpretation ('let him that readeth understand'), Luke decides to remove all possible obscurity by having Jesus say that such desolation will come when Jerusalem is surrounded by armies, and pagan ones at that (v. 24). Such alterations leave one in no doubt that Luke has modified his sources in the light of the fall of Jerusalem in AD 70. By the standards of twentieth-century historical writing this must look like some kind of deceit, with Jesus's 'prophecy' deliberately modified to suit subsequent events. But, as I tried to show when looking at Old Testament prophecy, its concern was never with precise prediction. Probably all Jesus ever intended to say was that the desecration of Jerusalem was inevitable given the obduracy of its people (cf. Mark 13:9–13). Luke was then simply making explicit for the reader that this had now happened, and so now no longer lay in the future, as something still to be awaited and feared.

But from looking at the way in which particular short sections have been adapted to suit the needs of the community, it is but a short step to asking how the evangelist has done this with his Gospel as a whole (the theme of redaction criticism). It is this question which has dominated post-war study, and precisely because it is not yet fully resolved, it is one in which the theology student can take full part. But it is interesting not just because it is a discussion still in transition, but also because it raises fundamental questions not just about how the evangelists use their material but equally as much about how we should use the Bible today.

One temptation the modern reader has when first encountering the Gospels is to suppose that their nearest equivalents are biographies. Of course they are biographies of a sort, but it is only when we appreciate how different the rules were for writing biography – and indeed history in general – in the ancient world that we shall get anywhere near the truth. There are two key features of ancient biography that need to be remembered. First, the primary rationale for organizing material in writers like Plutarch, Arrian, Philostratus and Diogenes Laertius was by *topic*, not chronologically. Secondly, there seems to have been almost no interest in psychological development, the preoccupation of so much modern biography. Instead, and surprisingly to us, character was conceived of statically and deeds and words were thought sufficient to reveal who the person was. Then, if we take history in the wider sense, two further points can be made. First, history was expected to edify, and so both the typical Jewish and pagan reader would expect to learn something of relevance to themselves and their lives. This should be obvious from our discussion earlier of Old Testament histories, but the same applied in the pagan world. Tacitus, for example, expected his readers to detect the way in which the absolute power of the Emperor corrupted everything. Secondly, even the attribution of the sort of thing someone *might* have said, rather than what he actually said, was widely recognized as justified. So, for example, that most careful of ancient historians Thucydides opens his *History* by remarking that, given the limitations of his sources, 'my method has been. . . . to make the speakers say what in my opinion was called for by each situation.' By comparison it is in fact quite unlikely that the synoptics took the same degree of liberty in what they ascribed to Jesus. Rather, they were working within an already existing tradition of what he said. But of course, as we have already noted, there is another sense in which they took greater liberties, in their desire to bring out the relevance of what he had said to their own times. So perhaps the difference could be put by saying that, whereas Thucydides freely composed in order to make the past intelligible, the synoptics freely adapted to make sure that the past continued to speak to the present.

With these points behind us, we are in a better position to appreciate redaction criticism. What it has disclosed is the extent to which all the evangelists have organized their material to make theological and not just historical points. In attempting to achieve this they take liberties that today we would regard as unacceptable but which become readily intelligible in the context of the ancient world. However, one should not think that such editing (redaction means editing) to produce a particular reaction in one's readers has ceased in the modern world. Far from it! A useful exercise would be to take a number of different newspapers' reports of the same news item, and compare them. As a result one will soon see that the selection and presentation of material to make a point is by no means a lost art. Indeed, precisely because of the limited number of the synoptic sources, in some ways they represent a more controlled and moderate use than their modern counterparts.

There are two reasons why I find the particular types of questions raised by redaction criticism especially fascinating. First, it clearly reveals the variety of types of approach that are possible to the phenomenon of Jesus's life, death and resurrection. It is very easy to see one's acceptance or rejection of the Bible as dependent on accepting one particular 'party-line', as it were, whereas what we in fact discover is the reactions of very different sorts of individuals, each making Jesus their own, yet still in a way that is only explicable in terms of them responding to one and the same Lord. Secondly, the fact that their response varied in part because of their different circumstances raises and legitimizes the same question for the contemporary Church, and indeed for every generation. This is certainly one of the main lessons to be learned from the history of the Church, that the message of the Bible has never remained static, but has always been in process of adaptation to the needs of the existing community.

Four perspectives on Jesus

One way for the reader to discover how redaction works in detail would be by looking at some professional practioners of the art, for instance the classic three, Willi Marxsen on Mark, Hans Conzelmann on Luke and Günther Bornkamm on Matthew. But at the earlier stages of study probably rather more would be gained by attempting the task oneself. First sit down and read each of the Gospels in turn, noting what salient features strike you, and what you are surprised to find omitted. Then by use of a synopsis (where the three Gospels are set out with similarly worded passages in parallel columns), try in the light of what you have already noted to produce possible reasons for the changes made. It is a very revealing exercise, no matter how much of a novice one is. I am no New Testament scholar, but in what follows I shall draw attention to some of the differences I find particularly intriguing.

Luke, as we have already noted, was not the earliest gospel. But it does provide clear evidence of the later Church's willingness to respond to very different historical circumstances. For, whether part of Jesus's original teaching or not, the early Church had certainly been dominated by an apocalyptic sense of the imminence of the coming of God's kingdom. Paul for instance had declared that 'the time is short' (cf. I Cor. 7:29). However, as the years passed, the Church was required to adapt to the new circumstances, in which the imminent end of the world seemed delayed or postponed.

Luke provides one illustration of this adaptation, just as 2 Peter 3:8 ('One day is with the Lord as a thousand years, and a thousand years as a day') represents another. Instead, Luke so structures his Gospel and its sequel, Acts, as to emphasize that we are now living in a third major dispensation or Age after the time of Israel and the life of Jesus, namely that of his Church. Thus, while Mark had ended his account in open-ended expectation of the Parousia or Second Coming (his Gospel originally ended at 16:8), Luke has Paul at the end of Acts in Rome, with the mission of the Church going out to all the world. And so to emphasize our role in this world as distinct from concentrating all our hopes on another, he does not hesitate to change the emphasis in Jesus's reply to the High Priest. For whereas Mark had 'you will see the Son of Man seated at the right hand of power, and coming with the clouds of heaven' (14:62) Luke makes this a present reality (which of course from the perspective of Christian faith it is): 'from now on the Son of Man shall be seated at the right hand of the power of God (Luke 22:69). Again, because this leads him to see a continuing plan of God in history going through Judaism to the growth of the Church, he even changes the feel of

Mark's geography to make the point. Thus, while Mark had contrasted Galilee and Jerusalem with the latter being seen as the place of Jesus's rejection and the source of opposition to him (cf. 3:22), and Galilee as the despised part of Palestine from which the gospel would move away from Judaism, Luke insists that the Church has absorbed what is worth while in Judaism and gone beyond it. So significantly his Gospel, unlike Mark's, opens and closes in the Temple, while to make this theological point he even takes the liberty of changing the announcement at the tomb (24:6, contrast Mark 16:7) so that he can make Jesus's appearances in Jerusalem central to his account rather than those in distant, peripheral Galilee. Of course, one must not jump to the conclusion that all differences from Mark are thus theologically motivated. Luke also seems to have had access to some independent traditions, and so, while the appearance of two figures rather than one at the tomb might have a theological motive, the fact that John independently also has two points in a different direction, as does Luke's recording of the presence of different women from Mark. So, though the sorts of historical restraints exercised are rather different from those in the modern world, that does not mean that we are ever dealing with pure invention. It is just that some historial details are not thought to matter particularly in relation to the more important issue of Jesus's significance, and I must admit I agree.

But omissions can sometimes be as significant as inclusions. For many Protestant Christians the atonement, a doctrine of the significance of Christ's death, is regarded as the heart of the Christian faith – and indeed for some at the more fundamentalist end of the spectrum, a particular theory, the penal view, at that. If one looks at the New Testament as a whole, particularly through the eyes of St Paul, one might well come away with the thought that one had no other choice. But in Luke in fact we find someone more concerned to stress the less stark side of the Christian faith. So in a speech attributed to Paul on the Areopagus Hill in Athens, we discover not the characteristic Pauline emphases, but rather God addressing himself to the whole world through the natural order, and culminating in the life and resurrection of Jesus, but in a way such that no mention is even made of his cruel death (Acts 17:24–31). Similarly in his Gospel one of the best-known verses in Mark, 'The Son of Man came not to be served, but to serve, and to give his life a ransom for many' (10:45), is modified through omission of the last phrase. Instead all we have is: 'I am in the midst of you as he that serveth' (22:27). It is almost as though Luke represents the typical layman, impatient of abstract theological thinking: instead, he says let's get on with the purely practical task of following Jesus's example of service, and in particular service to the outcast and downtrodden. This is perhaps the explanation of so many of the compassionate stories and incidents unique to his Gospel – including the parable of the prodigal son (15:11–32), the parable of the rich man and Lazarus (16:19–31), the woman who was a sinner (7:37–50), the plea for forgiveness for those organizing the Crucifixion and his words to the penitent thief (23:34 and 43), the story of the Pharisee and the publican (18:9–14) and the incident of Zacchaeus (19:1–10), which typically concludes with the comment that 'The Son of Man came to seek and to save that which was lost.'

By contrast Matthew's Gospel seems much sterner stuff, what with the enormously high ethical demands of the Sermon on the Mount combined with the recurring reference to the threat of hellfire. In fact, on this last matter Matthew is markedly out of step with the other Gospels. Thus his six references to hell, six to 'weeping and gnashing of teeth' and three to 'outer darkness', far surpass the number of allusions in the other Gospels. 'Weeping and gnashing of teeth' only occurs once elsewhere (Luke 13:28), and 'outer darkness' not at all. The fact that hell (Gehenna) is actually the name of a valley outside Jerusalem where human sacrifice by fire had been practised raises the question of how far anything more than a dramatic metaphor for the consequences of sin as alienation from God is intended. In a similar way a modern poet like T. S. Eliot can use the image of fire in *The Four Quartets* to express the starkness of the choices confronting us in life: 'being consumed by fire or fire'. But, whatever the point, what we can say is this. Since the imagery is in both Mark and Q it must go back to Jesus himself, though Matthew has clearly decided to give it far greater prominence than would have been justified by his sources. This is sometimes taken as illustrative of Matthew's attempt to bludgeon his readers into acceptance, but whether that is so or not it also illustrates the seriousness with which he regarded the Christian's call to lead a very different sort of life.

Indeed, the injunction unique to Matthew, 'Be ye perfect, even as your Father which is in heaven is perfect' (5:48), might be taken as summing the entire spirit of his Gospel. Intriguingly, Luke in his nearest parallel passage has: 'Be ye merciful, even as your Father is merciful' (Luke 6:36). The passages are not sufficiently close for us to conclude that one or other evangelist has altered the text of Q (cf, Matt. 5:43–8 and Luke 6:27–8 and 32–6). But they do illustrate beautifully the very different emphases which attracted them to the gospel, with Luke as usual reaching out in forgiveness to others and Matthew taking the gospel as a challenge to holiness in his own life-style. Thus Matthew's polemic against the Pharisees on the one hand and on the other his insistence that not one jot or tittle shall pass from the law (5:18) should probably be interpreted as a rather difficult balancing act in terms of which Jesus is seen as deepening the requirements and challenges of the moral aspects of the Jewish law rather than simply abrogating them.

This call to perfection, the need to 'hunger and thirst after righteousness', is in fact a recurring theme of Matthew's Gospel. What he finds wrong with his fellow Jews is not their laws, but the fact that they make them finite and all too possible of realization – instead of being challenged by the teaching of Jesus, not to deny these laws, but to carry them a stage further into a more ideal, more challenging morality.

It is with Matthew that we associate the declaration that 'Till heaven and earth pass away, one jot or one tittle shall in no wise pass away from the law' (5:18). This is often interpreted as implying some new sort of legalism. That the phrase was original to Jesus, there can be no doubt, since it is also found in Luke, though in a very different context (16:17), where it can easily pass unnoticed, and in fact it is clear that Luke could not quite see what Jesus was getting at. But

Matthew at least has fully grasped the point, and indeed precisely because of this carefully corrects his sources to make sure that it won't be misunderstood.

So, for example, Mark's account of Jesus's attitude to the sabbath is very easy to read with the implication that now no rules whatsoever are to attach to sabbath observance, whether it be the duty to rest or to attend church. To avoid such an interpretation, Matthew omits Jesus's words 'The sabbath was made for man, and not man for the sabbath' and instead supplements Mark's account of Jesus's teaching with additional material, showing that what Jesus had in mind was not the denial of sabbath obligations but the insistence that they be set in a wider context in which other obligations and ideals might have to take precedence (cf. Mark 2:23–8 and Matt. 12:1–8). In other words, while a reading of Mark might allow one to think that there might be occasions when one had no obligations, for Matthew what Jesus is saying is that at no point in one's life can one escape the challenge of the gospel – it's always calling one to do something, sometimes something small for God, sometimes something great, but never nothing. And that too is why the comment about not a jot or tittle passing from the law is immediately followed by the injunction: 'Except your righteousness exceed that of the scribes and Pharisees, ye can in no wise enter the Kingdom of Heaven.'

But are not such standards all too much to bear? No, says Matthew, because they are always balanced by Jesus's message of forgiveness, as illustrated in the story that may well have helped to give this Gospel its name, that of Matthew the publican. The author was not the apostle Matthew – for why then would he have needed to use two other Gospels as sources, Mark and Q? But the Gospel has still got something to do with someone called Matthew since the author substitutes Matthew instead of Levi as the name of the publican or tax-gatherer whom Jesus called (cf. Mark 2:14; Matt. 9:9), and he reinforces this identification by referring to Matthew in the list of apostles not just as Matthew but as 'Matthew the publican' (cf. Mark 3:18; Matt. 10:3). While it could just be an additional piece of factual information, one suspects that something more is at stake, and that this is the author's way of emphasizing that the community must have no limits to its membership, with not even those who have collaborated with the Roman occupying power by collecting taxes on its behalf excluded from the divine forgiveness. Indeed, there is quite a lot of teaching about forgiveness that is unique to Matthew. For example, he alone supplements the Lord's Prayer by adding a comment of Jesus that there can be no forgiveness unless one forgives in turn (6:14–15). So there is no real conflict with Luke. It is just that concern for the outcast and marginalized is not given as central a place.

But if the central distinctive message of Matthew is not too difficult to ascertain, this is not to say that no puzzles remain. Indeed, even Bornkamm found some of his ideas on Matthew undergoing a sommersault between 1956 and 1970. Thus in the former year he was arguing from the discussion of the Temple tax in 17:24–7 that Matthew's community must still have been paying it as practising Jews, while by 1970 he was using the following chapter (18:19–20) to argue that though the community was small it knew itself to be cut off from Judaism. Whether one can deduce that much from either passage seems questionable, but by constantly raising questions we may at least sometimes make progress towards answers. However, it is almost as important sometimes to choose the right type of question. One can illustrate this from Matthew's description of the earthquake at the time of the Crucifixion (27:51–3). If one asks the purely historical question of whether it happened, one is likely to conclude that since it is not in the other three Gospels and given its character, it is likely to be just a legendary accretion, as so many commentaries conclude. But that is really to ignore the more important issue of what motivated Matthew to include it, and this time something much more interesting emerges. For one can see that it has the same motivation as the rather obscure verse in I Peter 3:19 which speaks of the resurrected Christ preaching to 'the spirits in prison'. That verse eventually gave rise to the phrase in the Apostles' Creed about Christ descending to hell (meaning thereby 'the place of departed spirits'). But, whether one speaks of Christ going down to Hades to preach the gospel as in Peter or of the spirits coming out of their graves to share in the good news as in Matthew's description of the earthquake, the same theological point is being made, even if by admittedly very different symbolic language: Christ's resurrection brings with it salvation for *all* people, for the dead as much as for the living. So it is part of Matthew's claims for the cosmic significance of Christ.

Nor should we think of Matthew alone indulging in this way of thinking. When Mark writes (15:38) that when Jesus died 'the veil of the Temple was rent in twain from the top to the bottom', one misses the point if one makes the historical question primary. Of course some New Testament scholars have been silly enough to deny the miraculous out of hand, like Bultmann. I for one certainly believe that miracles happen and that the Resurrection, the way in which Jesus continued to be alive after death, was one such. Equally in this case I find no difficulty in believing that God damaged the temple curtain in this way. But that is not the key issue, eithe for us or for Mark. What matters is that the old order which insisted that only the High Priest once a year could pass behind that curtain to enter the most holy sanctuary of Judaism has now been for ever broken for the Christian through Christ giving him direct access to God. Of course, some miracles in the Bible would quite lose their point if they had not happened. Indeed, unless some of Jesus's miracles happened – including the Resurrection – it is hard to see how supreme significance could ever have been attached to him; but this is quite different from supposing that their literal truths are all equally significant for belief. Indeed, one has quite failed to understand what Matthew and Mark are saying in these - instances of the earthquake and Temple curtain until one has gone beyond the literal question to that of their symbolic significance.

However, most of Mark is not like that. It is shot through with the miraculous without any symbolic significance being intended, and it seems to have been precisely the strangeness of Jesus that attracted Mark to him. So, instead of his teaching, Mark very much concentrates on Jesus's actions. Jesus suddenly emerges, full-stage as it were, as a grown adult, preaching that the Kingdom of God is at hand. But we are given next to no information regarding what this kingdom is about, apart from the fact that it will require of us repentence for our sins and that in Jesus's person it is coming with great authority and great power. For, as Mark records, everything normally beyond human control obeys him – the wind, the waters and the demons (who were then thought of as lying behind so much illness). But who is this puzzling figure with such power? Mark offers us no clear, unambiguous answer. Thus the strange title, Son of Man, is left unexplained, and the central declaration of Jesus as the Christ right at the mid-point of the Gospel is almost immediately subverted as having any simple, straightforward meaning by Jesus's response: 'Get behind me, Satan' (8:29–33). Then comes the horrific death of this man of power, followed by a mysteriously incomplete resolution. For, while he records Jesus's triumph over death in the sense that he mentions the empty tomb, Mark's Gospel originally ended abruptly at 16:8 without any mention of the Resurrection appearances. Instead, he simply states the terror and awe with which the discovery was made that the tomb was empty. It is perhaps little wonder that a later editor felt it necessary to add a brief account of the Resurrection itself.

But for Mark the purpose of his Gospel was clearly to raise interest, not to give answers. Any reader cannot help but ask himself who is this strange, enigmatic figure, who exercised such power but who none the less chose to die in such a hideous way. The Gospel originally ended in the way it did because, no doubt, it provides yet one more pressure on the reader to seek some further explanation from within the Christian community itself.

Though nowadays there is increasing recognition that Mark is as theological in his purposes as the others, there is still no agreement as to what these purposes were. This is hardly surprising as in his case we do not have his sources with which to make comparisons, though there is widespread recognition that many of these sources could have been written. At any rate this would help to explain why there are so many doublets in his Gospel, and also the reintroduction of the same figure twice within the same story. For instance in Mark 9: 14–29 the crowd is introduced twice (vs. 14 and 25), and the boy (17 and 20), while the same spirit is called once 'dumb' and once 'unclean' (17 and 25). Conflicting interpretations about Mark's theological purposes are legion. Was the Gospel intended to represent a cosmic battle between God and supernatural forces of evil with Christ as God's agent, and does this explain the alien character it has for many of us? Or does it represent an attack on all triumphalist christologies and so does Matthew perhaps represent a counter-blast? Or is the incomprehension of the disciples supposed to represent the reader and so be an invitation to self-criticism? New Testament scholarship has so far not taken us beyond these questions.

John is different again. Bultmann did much to establish the existence of sources in John, though his attempt to identify influences from Greek rather than Palestinian ideas received a major setback when the contrasts between light and darkness that he had sought to explain were found to have already existing Palestinian precedents in the newly discovered Dead Sea Scrolls. Indeed, today there is increasing recognition of the historical value of the independent traditions that have helped shape the narrative content of this Gospel. To give but one instance, almost all scholars would think that the three-year ministry suggested by this Gospel is inherently more plausible than the brief one-year activity described by the synoptics. Again, given the interrogation before Pilate that precedes the Crucifixion, John is more likely to be right than Mark that the latter began at noon rather than 9.00 a.m. (John 19:14; Mark 15:25), though it is important to add that both mention the time not for historical reasons but for symbolic ones. John's intention is to alert his readers to the fact that Jesus is the true Passover Lamb, unlike the lambs being sacrificed for Passover at that same moment. Mark wants his readers to think of Amos 8:9 ('I will make the sun go down at noon and darken the earth in broad daylight) when Jesus finally dies three hours later at noon (Mark 15:33): darkness then falls just as on the decisive Day of the Lord spoken of by Amos. Yet one should add that such symbolic concerns seem always to have operated within strict limits. For, though both use their material in this way what is none the less striking is the extraordinary degree to which these two independent sources agree about the general pattern of events during Jesus's passion. Thus, though no doubt irritating to the modern historian, it seems as though they correctly perceived that some facts matter, whereas others do not and so can without distortion be manipulated to suit these symbolic concerns. That Jesus was crucified and why he was crucified matter; the precise time of day does not.

But this general uniformity between the synoptics and St John in the outline of events fails to find a parallel echo in the content of Jesus's teaching. In the former, Jesus preaches in parables and short, pithy sayings, whereas in John we have long discourses. John is in fact unique among the evangelists in telling us that he is using symbolic language, in that he describes each of the seven major miracles of his Gospel as a 'sign'. For instance, the point of recounting the turning of water into wine is not to draw attention to the fact that Jesus produced so much wine at his first miracle that all the guests must have had a hangover (at least 100 gallons according to 2:6), but to emphasize that Jesus came to bring the wine of new life into the world out of the old order of Judaism with its purificatory jars (which had been used for the miracle). So a less historical use for Jesus's words was perhaps to have been expected. At any rate what seems to have happened is that he has used elements of what Jesus had said in order to build up through the speeches a fuller account of who he really was. So, for example, Jesus's talk to Nicodemus about the need for new birth (John 3:1–8) echoes Jesus's historical assertion about the need to become as a little child (Matt. 18:3). The language about Jesus as the good shepherd in chapter 10 develops the historical Jesus's parable about the shepherd who cares for the lost sheep (Luke 15). Again, John's description of Jesus's intimacy with his Father is but an elaboration of the earthly Jesus's sense of intimacy as exhibited in his use of Abba, the Aramaic for 'Dad', when referring to his Father (Mark 14,36), and his authoritative language in the Sermon on the Mount and elsewhere ('But I say unto you'). It also echoes the so-called Johannine thunderbolt that is to be found in both Matthew and Luke: 'Everything has been entrusted to me by my Father; and no one knows the Son except the Father, just as no one knows the Father except the Son and those to whom the Son chooses to reveal him' (Matt. 11:27; Luke 10:22). Even the dialogue in chapter 8 that discusses who has the right to call themselves Abraham's children and which culminates in a declaration of Christ's divinity – 'Before Abraham was, I am' – can be seen to have its antecedents in the historical Jesus's discussion of what it is to be a child of Abraham. Jesus taught that only those who are faithful and loving will take their places alongside Abraham in the feast of the Kingdom (cf. Matt. 8:11–12; Luke 16:19–31).

Of course we no longer take such liberties, but arguably in terms of the rules of the time it was a quite brilliant solution to a major difficulty that confronted all the evangelists. It was only in the light of the Resurrection that the young Church began to understand properly who Jesus really was. But, if that is so, what alternative had they but to rewrite the story to some degree so that as it was being told its true significance could be brought out? All historical writing, even modern history, does this to some degree. The agreement in 1938 between Hitler and the British Prime Minister, Chamberlain, only became a weak compromise in the light of what happened; at the time it was hailed as a great success – 'peace in our time'. Yet almost all historians writing an account of the history of the Second World War will describe Munich as it is now *retrospectively* seen to be. So even in purely modern terms it is possible to make sense of what led the author to write in the way he did. Whether he was justified in so doing is of course quite another matter. Since this book is only intended as an introduction to theology, this is not the place to go into the issue in any great detail, but some preliminary comments about the relationship between the historical Jesus and the Christ preached by the Gospels would seem apposite.

And what of Jesus himself?

So far we have been examining the impact of Jesus as reflected in the four Gospels, and how they need to be read. Throughout I have stressed that, though they make major alterations to the previous tradition, these are never arbitrary. The rules may not be our own, but the authors are always guided by the desire to make explicit what they believe to have been already implicit in what they have inherited. This gives good grounds for confidence that the events and sayings in the Gospels in essence go back to the life of Jesus himself. In fact the only major challenge to traditional understandings would seem to come on the question of Jesus's self-consciousness. The disparity between John and the synoptics on this matter makes it extremely unlikely that Jesus ever claimed to be God, while the application of form criticism to the synoptics had led some scholars, including Bultmann, to question whether he even thought of himself as the Messiah. A related question is whether some of his language about the Kingdom of God (e.g. Mark 9:1) implies that he believed in the imminence of a new age that ultimately failed to dawn. Even on such issues as this it seems to me that New Testament scholarship has been positively beneficial in helping the believing Christian to understand better the true nature of the Incarnation. But before illustrating why this might be so, I shall put the point more broadly, since it seems to me that historical investigation of the New Testament has in fact brought with it in general *increased* grounds for confidence, not less.

In 1984 Independent Television in Britain showed a series of programmes entitled 'Jesus: The evidence'. What was intriguing about them was the way in which non-believers just as much as believers can exhibit irrational insecurity in their approach to the subject. For they were clearly directed by someone who felt it necessary to bring on stage all the more bizarre types of theory about Christian origins – nocturnal cults and the rest. Space was even devoted to the claim that Jesus had never existed, something utterly implausible given not only the difficulty of then explaining the rise of Christianity but also the references in pagan as well as Christian first-century writers to his existence.

In fact the truth is that as historical investigation has advanced, the documents have increasingly come to be seen as more reliable, not less. An excellent illustration of this is the contrast between nineteenth- and twentieth-century declarations on the subject. The two most famous New Testament scholars of the nineteenth century, David Friedrich Strauss and Ferdinand Christian Baur, both placed the Gospels well into the second century, the latter in fact suggesting that St John was totally without historical value, while Bruno Bauer assigned all of Paul's Epistles to the reign of Marcus Aurelius, that is between 161 and 180.

Contrast this with the situation today. Take, for example, the text itself. In the nineteenth century our earliest text of the New Testament dated from the fourth century AD and the earliest text of the Old from the ninth. But in the 1930s various papyri fragments of the New Testament began to be discovered in the sands of Egypt, pushing back our knowledge of the text two centuries and, in the case of one fragment of John, chapter 18, the so-called P52, to AD 125. Then in 1947 came the discovery of the Dead Sea Scrolls that pushed our knowledge of the Old Testament text a thousand years earlier, into the first century BC. Now to the modern mind this may not sound particularly impressive, since the manuscripts are still not contemporaneous. But one needs to bear two facts in mind: first, these twentieth-century discoveries have demonstrated the essential reliability in the transmission of the texts; secondly, one needs to set this picture against the situation in the ancient world generally. For example, one of our main sources for the history of the Roman Empire is Tacitus' *Annals*, but the two manuscripts on which we must rely in this case date from well over a thousand years later than the time of Tacitus. So the biblical historian is in this respect much better off than the secular.

Equally if we turn to content there are grounds for increasing confidence. There is only the space here to give two examples at random. It used to be fashionable to follow F. C. Baur and deny John's Gospel any historical value. Indeed, if you had read any critical commentary on John 5 prior to the First World War, almost certainly you would have been informed that the reference to the Pool of Bethesda with its five colonnades was symbolical and not historical. No known pool in the ancient world had five colonnades and in any case no sense could attach to how the odd number would be distributed. But between the two world wars archaeologists rediscovered this Pool and all became clear. There had in fact been two pools, with a fifth colonnade running between them.

So St John can in this case be seen as preserving a reliable, independent tradition. Again, the discovery of the heretical Gospel of Thomas at Nag Hammadi in 1945 with its parallels to Q but no conceivable relationship of dependency on Matthew or Luke established beyond doubt the existence of a collection of Jesus's sayings that antedates these Gospels.

While it remains difficult to determine precisely when the Gospels were written, no one now takes seriously the views of those nineteenth-century scholars I mentioned earlier. Indeed, already towards the end of that century J. B. Lightfoot's successful dating of the Apostolic Fathers (a group of early Christian, non-biblical writers who often refer to the Gospels) to the 90s of the first century and the early second century meant that we had a firm latest date for the Gospels themselves. More uncertain is the earliest possible date. Though there are occasional defenders of very early dating (for example, John Robinson), most scholars take Luke 21:20 to have been rewritten in the light of the fall of Jerusalem in 70, while its original in Mark 13:14 is thought to be sufficiently vague for it to antedate thes traumatic events.

Bruno Bauer's views about the late date of Paul would now universally be regarded as absurd. For long it had been thought that I Thessalonians was the first of all Paul's letters. It was even known from internal evidence at what stage of Paul's career he must have written it. For, taking this epistle, I Corinthians chapter 3 and Acts 17–18 together, we can deduce that Paul wrote I Thessalonians near the beginning of an eighteen-month stay at Corinth. But when was that? Acts 18 tells us that after he had been there some considerable time someone called Gallio became pro-consul of the area, Achaia, and Paul was brought for examination before him. But for two millennia no one knew when Gallio was Governor of Achaia and so the information was of little help until earlier this century an inscription was found at Delphi which enables us to date the beginning of Gallio's pro-consulship exactly to AD 51, with the letter written the year before, less than twenty years after Christ's death.

But, as mentioned earlier, there is another side to advances in New Testament criticism that many a believing Christian still finds disconcerting, and that is the way in which Jesus is presented as having a much more human, fallible consciousness. In particular he does not seem to have thought of himself as God, and may even have thought that the world was coming to an end. Of course, for some people what appeals about Jesus is precisely his purely human qualities, and for them Christ's divinity will be seen as something better discarded as an unnecessary dogmatic accretion. But probably for most Christians such a belief remains integral to their faith, and so it is worth spending a little time to outline how it can remain defensible despite all these changes in our knowledge.

St John's Gospel is unequivocal in its assertion of Christ's divinity. Thus it opens in its first verse with an emphatic declaration that the Word who became flesh (1:14) was God, and throughout one has on Jesus's lips the claim to be one with God, including for example the declaration that: 'Before Abraham was, I am' (8:58). This is an allusion to the meaning of the name 'Yahweh' as revealed to Moses in Exodus 3 (v. 14), and so there can be no doubt that the author intended to equate Jesus and God, though, even if there had been, all uncertainty is removed with Thomas's confession before the resurrected Lord: 'My Lord and my God' (20:28). But the situation is very different in the synoptics. Jesus's teaching is almost wholly about the Kingdom of God rather than about himself, while even the titles used of him do not imply as much as was once thought. So, for instance, we now know that 'Son of God' implies a special rather than a unique relationship with God and that it was in fact ancient Israel's way of conceiving the special bond that existed between God and the King (cf., for example, Ps. 2:7; 2 Sam. 7:14). Nor was it unique in the Middle East in using such language, since parallels exists in Assyrian descriptions of their monarch. Nor will it do to suggest that the phrase had narrowed its significance by the time of Jesus to carry something of the implication of divinity, as in Greek thought. For, while such a claim might have once been possible, evidence from the Dead Sea Scrolls has conclusively shown that it was commonly taken simply to refer to the coming Davidic Messiah. When one adds to this the slow recognition in Mark of him even as Messiah (8:29) and contrasts this with the immediate acknowledgement of him as the sacrificial Lamb of God in John (1:36), it is hard to resist the conclusion that John and the synoptics cannot both be historically correct.

But it would be a mistake to jump from this to the easy conclusion that John's descriptions are therefore unjustified. For one most reckon with the fact that all Paul's letters were written between AD 50 and his execution in Rome, sometime between 62 and 67, and that already in these letters, written thus *before* the synoptics, divine functions comparable to those in John are already being ascribed to Jesus. So for instance in I Corinthians he is described as having complete authority over all things (cf. 15:24–8), in Philippians as being 'in the form of God' and 'equal with God' (2:6), while the opening chapter of Colossians (v 15–17) assigns him the same role in creation as was later accorded him by the opening chapter of John. So it just will not do to suggest that the 'divinization' of Christ is a late development. For it clearly antedates the synoptics, though they show less evidence of it than the earlier Paul.

This is not the place to discuss the matter in any detail, but a likely explanation compatible with a doctrine of Incarnation is this: Paul fully reflects the experience of the *post*-Resurrection Church, while the synoptics, because they are trying to describe the *pre*-Resurrection life of Jesus, display a largely unresolved tension between fulfilling that task and ensuring that the reader is left in no doubt as to the status that Jesus now enjoys. In other words, what I am suggesting is something like the following scenario. As Mark's account of Jesus's identification as the Messiah implies, it was only gradually during his lifetime that his disciples became aware of what kind of status he enjoyed. It is unclear how far this had got by the time of his death, but, however far, it was completely transformed by the experience of Jesus still being alive after death and all the powers that now accrued to him. In their attempt to describe that experience, the incipient Church ransacked language in its attempts to find words adequate to the task, and indeed even jettisoned titles used by Jesus himself as inadequate to the purpose. The writings of Paul reflect that early experience, as indeed in the abandonment of the early title for Christ, 'Son of

Man'. But Paul's task was an easier one than that of the synoptics, for he only indirectly refers to the life and teaching of Jesus, and nowhere does he seek to justify the role he gives to Christ from Jesus's own words. By contrast the synoptics seem to have seen their primary role as the recording of the life and teaching of Jesus, with only relatively minor adjustments to ensure applicability to their own age, of the kind illustrated earlier in this chapter. Some liberties were also taken to indicate his significance, as with Matthew's organization of the teaching material into five blocks to hint that a greater than Moses is here. But it is only really with John that the bull is taken firmly by the horns, and this is why his Gospel is nearest in feel to what Paul says of Jesus. For, perhaps meditating on original words of Jesus (as in the examples I gave earlier), John transforms them almost out of recognition in his determination to make abundantly clear who this man is: God Incarnate. Of course the disciples may have been wrong in their perception of the Risen Christ. But it is worth remarking that that is a different issue from whether the development happened as I have just suggested, since there is no reason in principle why even an atheist should not accept that matters preceeded thus. There would then remain the further question of whether it was in fact a legitimate development.

Not all modern theologians are agreed that it was so. For them, John has claimed altogether too much, and all that is important about God's involvement with Jesus can be put much more simply. It is one of the perennial fascinations of theology to attempt to answer that question for oneself as one looks in detail at the life of Jesus and the early Church's experience of him as reflected in the New Testament. But an introduction can hardly tackle all the issues in a few pages; so suffice it to say that for me, at least, advances in New Testament scholarship have brought a deeper and richer understanding of the Incarnation. Far from it being a case of God appearing on earth supremely confident that nothing could really harm him, it was a complete entering into the human condition, with him fully becoming one with us, with all the temptations, anxieties and sufferings that involves. Paul is often thought to have borrowed from an earlier Christian hymn in Philippians 2. Whether so or not, it encapsulates admirably the Incarnation thus understood of one who 'being in the form of God. . .made himself of no reputation, and took upon him the form of a servant' (6–7).

But could such 'humility' (v. 8) have also involved believing that the world was about to end? Here too there have been major changes in our understanding of the life of Christ. Earlier generations tended to see Christ exclusively as an authoritarian teaching figure, preaching a timeless message. The first recognition of development and pluriform perspectives in the biblical material in the nineteenth century produced a reaction. The early Church was blamed for the authoritarian figure, whereas Jesus himself was depicted as preaching a gospel suspiciously like nineteenth-century liberalism itself, one entirely of love and tolerance. But increasingly that has had to give way to a much stranger figure, and now all New Testament scholars would be agreed that a phenomenon to which we have already referred when discussing the Old Testament, apocalyptic, played a key role in Jesus's ministry.

Albert Schweitzer (d. 1965) has numerous claims to fame – as missionary doctor working in his jungle hospital at Lambaréné in Gabon, as a brilliant organist and reinterpreter of Bach, or for his universally applied principle of 'reverence for life'. But among New Testament scholars his abiding status lies with a book he wrote before the First World War, *The Quest for the Historical Jesus*. In that work he attacks both liberal and traditional interpreters of Jesus for simply imposing their antecedent prejudices upon him. Instead, he argues, one must come to terms with a figure alien to both. For taking certain texts seriously (for example, Mark 9:1, 13:24–7; Matt. 10:23) means realizing that Jesus's ideas were much influenced by contemporary Jewish notions of eschatology, the imminent inauguration of the end of all things (the *eschaton*) by divine power. Schweitzer therefore suggests that Jesus expected God to inaugurate his Kingdom in his own lifetime and when these expectations were frustrated he decided to force the issue by going to Jerusalem and certain death.

The question has continued to be debated ever since. One example of a present-day scholar who continues to take this line is Ed Sanders, a proponent of 'restoration eschatology'. He argues that in Jesus's view the realization of the Kingdom was firmly attached to the destruction of the old Temple and building of a new. But there is no shortage of scholars who disagree. The best-known alternative to Schweitzer is perhaps that of C. H. Dodd (d. 1973), with his notion of 'realized eschatology', the idea that Jesus intended to speak of a Kingdom that is already being realised through his presence in the world. But, if a contemporary example is preferred, one might refer to the later writings of Norman Perrin or those of J. Francis Glasson and Bruce Chilton, all of whom choose to speak of what might be called a 'realizing eschatology', that Jesus did indeed think of a future Kingdom to be inaugurated by God but he had no definite timetable in mind.

Once more it would be absurd to arbitrate the issue in a sentence. Certainly the early Church thought that the end was imminent (cf., for example, I Cor. 7:29–31; Rom. 13:11). But this need not necessarily be explained by Jesus having had the same belief. For instance, it could have been the case that it was the pressure of the Resurrection experience that drew them to this conviction ('a new order must be dawning'), and this in turn might have led them to project back such a belief into Jesus's own life. Certainly there is a puzzle why, if this was such a central element in his teaching, it does so little to illuminate his teaching in general, or his parables in particular. So perhaps we should say that even if Jesus did think that the end was at hand it was not really what mattered to him. Rather what matters is how one stands now before God and in relation to one's neighbour.

Perhaps an analogy will help. The twentieth-century German atheist existentialist philosopher, Martin Heidegger, criticized the way in which most human beings seem simply to drift through life, following the herd. For him, living authentically meant living in the face of the inevitability of death and of the opportunities it opens up, as well as the limitations it imposes. Similarly, then, with Jesus. Becoming incarnate meant accepting the common assumptions of the time, such as the belief that the world was soon to end, and that Moses was the author of the Pentateuch (Mark 10: 3–4; Deut.

24:1–4). But for Jesus what really mattered in that belief was not the question of when God would bring the world to an end but the way in which it challenges us (like the inevitability of death which will come we know not when) to live each day as though it were our last. In other words, as in Heidegger's philosophy the important thing is not what is being said about the future but the way in which it challenges us to make a decision in the present.

THE BIBLE AS REVELATION

I promised to end this chapter with a few remarks on how God's role in all of this might best be understood. But before doing so let me first disabuse the reader of any lingering twentieth-century arrogance. For it is a common assumption that the Bible was universally interpreted in an entirely literal manner until Darwin and that only in our own day has a proper picture emerged of how it should be interpreted. As a matter of fact already in the third century AD Origen was objecting that it was absurd to suggest that our fate could literally have depended on eating the fruit of a forbidden tree, while in the following century Gregory of Nyssa rejected the idea that God could have literally hardened Pharaoh's heart or punished the first-born children of Egypt, since both involved unjust conceptions of punishment. This led both Origen and Gregory to seek for symbolic meanings. Indeed, as we shall note in the following chapter, throughout the Middle Ages other senses of Scripture were acknowledged and these were often seen as far more important than the literal. It is true that the Reformation brought more literalistic readings, but even in the nineteenth century the Danish theologian Søren Kierke- gaard published (in 1844 – fifteen years before Darwin's *Origin of Species*) a work entitled *The Concept of Anxiety* which insisted that the only intellible reading of the story of the Fall was a mythological one, which read it as the story of each and every one of us. So, while it remains true that the dominant reading remained a literal one, there was in fact greater diversity throughout the centuries than is commonly acknowledged. In fact our survey of the methods employed by biblical writers should already have given us pause for thought. For clearly they regarded something else as much more important than the mere passing on of the tradition. Its relevance to their own age had to be made explicit.

But if the use of Scripture by previous generations was much less wooden than its common caricature, they were still far behind us in their awareness of notions like change, progress and development. The tendency was to read texts as though they had been written in the present without due account being taken, for instance, of the way in which the meaning of words can change over the centuries. We have already encountered this problem in the case of the title 'Son of God'. But equally there was insufficient awareness of the way in which attitudes too can change over time. So, for example, it is only really in the twentieth century that we have come to appreciate that not all the Old Testament should be read as assuming monotheism, for in fact there are occasional passages (e.g. Ps. 86:8; 97:7-9) which imply the existence of other gods. Again, the story of Achan in Joshua 7, according to which not only he but his entire family is punished for an offence he alone has committed, is incompatible with the stress on individual responsibility that we find asserted in some of the prophets (Jer. 31:29; Ezek. 18:2). Another difficulty perhaps more familiar to the reader is the problem of reconciling some of the harsher pronouncements of the Old Testament with the stress on love in Jesus's teaching. An earlier generation (Augustine, Luther) would have said that the latter was really intended for individual action whereas the former provides guidance for the running of a state. Nowadays we are likely to recoil from the idea that some of the measures intended for captives in war could ever have been part of the divine will (e.g. Deut. 20:16; Ps. 137:9).

In such a situation it is hard to resist the conclusion that some of the doctrinal and moral statements in the Bible are not just inadequate but actually quite wrong, at least when set against the standards of later biblical perceptions. It is for reasons such as this, as well as the complexity of the documents as we now know them to be, that theologians have sought alternative models for revelation to the traditional one of God, as it were, simply dictating what we find on the page. One popular way of understanding God's involvement in the process is to say that this should be located in the events themselves (for example, the Exodus, the life of Jesus), while the Bible should be seen as human reflection on those divine acts. Another is to say that the Bible is simply intended as a vehicle towards an encounter with God and that there is therefore, properly speaking, no revelation until that personal engagement is accomplished.

For my part I find it helpful to begin with the awareness that God's activity in the Bible can now be seen to differ only in degree rather than kind from the way in which we experience him in our own lives. For one way of understanding the mixture of truth and falsehood in the Bible is to appreciate that as in our own case, so also with the biblical writers God has valued something more highly than the mere communication of his purposes, namely our freedom to come to accept them for ourselves. God is always there in our midst addressing us through the world he has created, through our consciences, through the community of faith to which we belong, through our own personal experience and through our conscious and unconscious reflection thereupon. But just as our perceptions of each other are clouded by antecedent assumptions, so also in the case of God. For example, people whose own lives are dominated by self-interest often find it impossible to believe in the altruism of others and it may take some very dramatic instance of another showing concern for them before this barrier is broken down. This is equally true of our everyday encounters. We very quickly pigeon-hole people and then respond to them on the basis of how we have labelled them, and it can often prove very difficult for the individual to get himself perceived in an alternative light. That being so, it is hardly surprising that any encounter with God should be fraught with precisely the same sort of difficulties, if it is truly the case that he leaves us free to determine our response to him. That God should be concerned with all humanity and not just with one's own nation (cf. Jonah) or that he should show no respect for merit (cf. Paul) are after all not easy truths to accept, far less the claim that God himself in Jesus followed the path of weakness and exposure to hurt. Little wonder then that it took centuries for the full nature of the character and purposes of God to become explicit even among those who professed to believe in him.

Instead, then, of viewing the biblical revelation as dictation, what I am suggesting is that one should see it more as God's dialogue with a particular community of faith, first with ancient Israel, then with the incipient Church. As in all free dialogue, the pace will have been set just as much by the ability of one partner to respond as by the other's desire to communicate. It is this fact which can make comprehensible the way in which ideas in the Bible develop, without at the same time undermining the authority of the book for the Christian. For it would remain true that earlier accounts of the nature and purposes of God would be declared deficient not against some arbitrary individual standard but by the hallmark of what the Bible itself had later to say on the subject.

Though there must be a strong sense in which for the Christian later must necessarily be better and therefore the New Testament be definitive in a way the Old could never be, one should not draw from this the conclusion that the new always supersedes what is old and makes it redundant. Sometimes, of course, it is: it is hard, for instance, to think of any contemporary relevance for the Book of Leviticus. But equally at times it is only by studying the past that we come properly to perceive the present. An example of this would be the use of the Exodus motif by contemporary Liberation theology in Latin America. For such attention to the Old Testament has made possible the recognition that in appropriate circumstances the gospel is just as much about political action as it is about personal transformation, whereas this insight might well have been lost had only the Gospels continued to be read, addressing as they do a situation of political powerlessness. Indeed, precisely because historical circumstances are always changing, different biblical books are likely to acquire special importance at different historical periods, as with John in the patristic period, Paul at the Reformation or Exodus for some contemporary theologians. And it is to a consideration of the sort of factors which have affected the history of the Church that we next turn.

3

A Changing Church

What makes its history interesting

I suspect that if a poll were conducted among students regarding the popularity of the various areas of theology, church history would come very low down the list in terms of its perceived importance and interest. This is a pity, as it seems to me to have a great deal to offer.

One reason for finding its study fascinating is connected with the title I have chosen to give this chapter. Continual change is a phenomenon which we have already encountered. Religion has always been responding to changed circumstances and that is why its expression occurs now in the form of myth, now in the form of various versions of the story of Moses, or now in the different emphases of the four Gospels. Of course this might mean that all we ever find is mere responses, but that would be to distort the facts. For arguably one of the major sources of the continuing strength of religion is its realization that one must change in order to remain the same. That is to say, because historical circumstances change, it is only by a religion being ready to alter its expression and emphasis that it can hope to preserve its essential content and message. So for instance it is arguable that increased stress on keeping the law was the only way of preserving Jewish religious identity in the face of the threats to the nation in the Exile and beyond, or that Christianity would not have survived had not unrealized eschatological hopes been transformed into new images as in Luke's third age of the Church or John's expression of it as an already existing reality (for example, John 17:3). So, similarly, in the history of the Church it is doubtful whether Christianity could ever have won the battle with the classical world had it not shown a willingness to translate its message into the terminology of pagan philosophy. Equally, without some attempt like the Reformation to come to terms with the new individualism of the Renaissance, it is hard to see how Christianity could have maintained its hold on western thinking for quite so long as it has. Discovering what adaptations have proved necessary (and why) is one of the sources of the study's interest.

But there are many others, including the challenging task of simply discovering what actually happened and why. I call it a challenging task because even when there is plenty of factual data available it is still no easy matter to step outside the prejudices and value system of one's own culture and environment and attempt a dispassionate judgement. It is sadly all too easy to impose the assumptions of one's own culture and age on a very different time and environment. Indeed, so extreme is the difficulty that the distinguished historian E. H. Carr has suggested in *What is History?* (1961) that the first question that one must always ask even of the modern historian is what his work tells us about the author himself: for instance, he points out the way in which the two major works which he used when studying the ancient world, Grote's *History of Greece* and Mommsen's *History of Rome*, tell us quite as much about their authors as they do about their respective periods. The former found reflected in ancient Athens his own ideals of liberal democracy, while the latter's disappointment over the failure of the 1848 revolution in Germany led him to desire a strong leader on the model of Julius Caesar. Yet there is no doubt that both were conscientious scholars, indeed great historians.

So we must always be on our guard against just projecting our own world view back in time, and the best way of ensuring that is to get to know really well the particular period we are studying. That means constantly asking questions and in particular asking whether the reasons which led people then to do certain things were necessarily the same as those that would motivate us now. To anticipate two examples which I shall discuss later, one would seriously misunderstand the nature of the early Church if one thought that the reasons for delaying baptism at that time were the same as apply today, just as one would miss the point of medieval interest in the grandparents of Jesus in resorting immediately to talk of medieval credulity or superstition.

Yet fascinating as this may be, to attempt to stand back and see things in the past as they actually were, it can also be deeply disconcerting, especially of course where the past continues to shape one's present. So, even forty years after the Second World War, to question whether the role of Churchill or Macmillan was an entirely honourable one still seems to many almost treasonable. It is therefore perhaps hardly surprising that in the field of religion – another area where, like national-ism, passions run strong – convictions can produce a distorting lens. Certainly it is salutary to recall how recent is the attempt of ecclesiastical historians to disengage themselves from auto-matic endorsement of a confessional perspective. Even as late as the beginning of this century the German historian Heinrich Denifle saw it as his duty to use his massive scholarship simply in order to demolish Martin Luther's reputation, as it was only really with the work of Joseph Lortz in 1939 that a change to a more balanced perspective among his fellow Roman Catholics began to emerge. I hasten to add that there is no shortage of similar examples in Protestantism, and indeed one contempor-ary church historian (John Kent) has questioned whether ideology has yet fully yielded to impartial assessment and so whether *The Unacceptable Face* does not still remain; hence the title of his book.

Yet, however difficult, the task remains a worthwhile one. For only thus will we be enabled to decide the significance to be attached to the continuing divisions within Christianity. To draw a parallel with architecture, the term 'Gothic' was originally coined at a time when more classical styles were all the rage to indicate contempt for the barbarism of the Middle Ages. For the Goths had been one of the tribes responsible for the collapse of the Roman Empire. But greater understanding in the late eighteenth and nineteenth centuries of what had motivated the medieval builders led to a complete re-evaluation of their work, with the movement known as the

'Gothic Revival' that has left such a marked imprint on English towns and cities. Indeed, many a contemporary medieval historian would want to carry the issue further and question the very label 'Middle Ages' – for it seems to have an inbuilt evaluation of the period as merely transitional.

In a similar way, for instance, current work on the Reformation is calling into question whether the traditional account of its significance is correct. The term itself makes one think of a radical new beginning, but increasingly it is the *continuities* that are being noted. Luther's individualism is seen as already prominent in the Renaissance, while the antecedents of many of his ideas have now been traced back to the philosophy dominant in the late Middle Ages. Indeed, if one takes elements in his thought such as his strong prejudice against the Jews, his lively belief in the reality of the Devil or his literalistic interpretation of Christ's presence in the Eucharist, one might well begin to ask what had changed. As we shall see, this has led some scholars to refuse to treat 1517 (the traditional date for marking the beginning of the Reformation) as in fact a key turning point in the religious history of Europe. Of course to some readers this will seem absurd because of the radical break with Rome that did occur. But one needs to recall that to take loyalty to the papacy as the test is already to make an evaluative judgement about how the nature of someone's religion is best defined, and it is by no means clear that theory on this matter always corresponds with practice.

Of course much more could be said on this issue (and much more *will* be said later in this chapter); but for the moment it is intended simply as one illustration of a more general point: the way which a fresh look at history can be used to challenge how we now perceive ourselves. Two other examples may be mentioned more briefly, just to underline the fact that the problem confronts the Catholic just as much as the Protestant. Both are taken from the nineteenth century. Papal infallibility was only declared as a dogma in 1870, and what the Roman Catholic has to come to terms with is the fact that this was under a pope (Pius IX) whose long pontificate was marked by resistance to change and unrelenting hostility to the modern world, as typified by his *Syllabus of Errors* of 1864 which among other things condemned rationalism, socialism and Bible societies, together with the view that there was any need for the pope to take account of 'progress, liberalism and modern civilisation'. Similarly those on the Anglo-Catholic side of the Church of England need to come to terms with the fact that one major reason for the success of its founding Oxford Movement was in the 1830s its coincidence with the Romantic Movement in society at large. The general archaizing tendency of Romanticism in reaction to industrialization made the Oxford Movement's appeal to the past particularly strong. In saying all of this I intend no comment on the merits of the Reformation, papal infallibility or the Oxford Movement. My sole purpose has been to indicate how challenging a task it can be to study their historical origins. Beliefs have never arisen in an historical vacuum, and so any adequate defence of them must always take this into account.

Thus there are three reasons for finding the study of church history fascinating. First, there is the way in which the Church has had to adapt to changed historical circumstances in order to stay the same. Secondly, there is the challenge it presents to us to try and see the world from the perspective of the participants then rather than just through our own spectacles now. Finally, there is the need to take history seriously if we are to offer not just propaganda but a plausible defence of what we hold most dear. Further illustrations of these points will emerge in what follows, but what I want to do now is move to specific periods of history, and give a few examples of the issues they raise. Particular attention will be devoted to the way in which historical assessments change. As some remarks will be made on the nineteenth century in chapter 4, I shall confine myself here to the early Church, the Middle Ages and the Reformation.

THE ENCOUNTER WITH PAGANISM

The first of these periods is often known as the patristic period after the Latin word for 'father'. That in itself is already – as with the term 'Middle Ages – to make an evaluative judgement, for in speaking of the period as informed by the writings of the 'Fathers' of the Church one is already implicitly making the claim that their 'fatherhood', the direction they gave the Church, is one which ought to be respected. That is a contention with which I would not seek to quarrel, but it is as well to remember that some of the most distinguished historians of the period have thought otherwise, including perhaps the most distinguished, Adolf Harnack (d. 1930), who saw the period essentially in terms of the corruption of the purity of the Gospel by Greek thought, in particular philosophy.

Certainly those first five centuries that hammered out agreed expressions of belief were decisive in shaping the claims of Christianity that were to be passed on to subsequent generations. So the importance of that period certainly cannot be denied. But here there is only space to illustrate the sort of issues raised, and how they might be debated. To that end I have selected two, one essentially historical, the other having possible theological ramifications.

What converted the Roman Empire?

Even modern pagans often think it obvious that Christianity had to succeed, so dismissive are they of ancient classical religion and its mythologies. But as I tried to demonstrate in the first chapter, mythology is not quite so easily dismissed. Others with more knowledge might put it all down to the fortuitous conversion of the Emperor Constantine in 312 but, as we shall see, its interpretation has proved far from straightforward. What I want to do here is not argue for a particular answer, but rather outline some of the difficulties encountered as one works one's way towards an answer.

The first thing that needs to be stressed is the unrivalled opportunities Christianity had during this period for the spread of the gospel, indeed arguably better than at any period until modern times. This is because all of the area round the Mediterranean, and much beyond (like England), was controlled by a single power and so facilities for travel were enormously enhanced. Not only was there no difficulty moving between what were to become the competing European states, but communications on land were much better organized than ever before and piracy on the high seas almost unknown. Not for nothing is the subsequent period known as the Dark Ages: for instance, the engineering achievements of the Romans were not matched again until the eighteenth century. Think of the network of Roman roads, bridges and aquaducts, or even their system of central heating.

Related to this point about ease of communications is one not often appreciated by students fresh to the period, and that is the sheer size of Roman cities. For instance, Rome itself is estimated to have had a population of one million people, which no European city was to match again until London passed this figure in the nineteenth century. In 1700 London had still only a population of just over half a million, and the next largest town in England was Norwich with a mere 30,000. After the fall of the Empire the population of Rome itself was to shrink to a figure not much larger than that mentioned for Norwich. Nor was Rome unique in having such a large concentration of people. Alexandria was almost certainly the second largest city with roughly half a million, and quite a number of cities probably exceeded the quarter of a million mark. These are all very rough estimates, but I mention them because it is so very much easier to pass information in towns than in the countryside. Poorer people lived in rather cramped conditions in the ancient equivalent of tower-blocks (*insulae*), while they had plenty of opportunities to meet in the market-place (*forum*) or when attending public shows. For instance, the Circus Maximus at Rome could accommodate 255,000 people and the Colosseum 45,000, while even the theatre at Ephesus into which Paul's companions were dragged (Acts 19:23–41) had a seating capacity of 24,000.

One further advantage needs to be mentioned and that is the Jewish Diaspora, that is, the spread of Jews throughout the world following the collapse of Jewish independence. For, given the fact that Christianity began as a sect of Judaism, this could not but help facilitate its transmission throughout the Empire. Thus out of Rome's million inhabitants it is estimated that perhaps between 40,000 and 50,000 were Jews, while in Alexandria it is known that two out of its five districts were predominantly Jewish and so the figure here could have reached as high as 200,000.

But, while it is easy thus to identify the opportunities Christianity had, it is much harder to estimate its success prior to the conversion of Constantine. Certainly Christianity spread quickly, for a mere thirty years after Jesus's death the pagan historian Tacitus can speak of there being 'large numbers' at Rome whom Nero could blame for the disastrous fire of 64. But one estimate suggests that only 2 per cent of the Empire was Christian in AD 250 (out of a possible total population of 250 million), while by the time of the Emperor's conversion it had only risen to 4 per cent. The truth is that we do not really know. Unlike the modern historian who would have plenty of government statistics available, all the ancient historian can do is generalize from a few isolated pieces of information. For instance, in assessing what percentage of the Empire was Christian in AD 250, we know that the church in Rome at this time supported 154 ministers of various kinds, as well as 'more than fifteen hundred widows and poor people'. But how many Christians should we infer from that number? And, even if we infer a higher figure than that proposed, what are we to make of other random facts that we know about the Empire? For example, we know that there was still no bishop or church in modern Split in Yugoslavia, though it was a town of sufficient importance for the Emperor Diocletian to build a palace for his retirement there. Again, archaeology has revealed that the synagogue at Dura Europos on the edge of the Empire (east of the Euphrates) was at this time still more impressive than the local Christian house-church.

All this of course changed with the conversion of Constantine, though not just at one fell swoop. The Edict of Milan of 313 granted toleration to Christianity but it was not until Theodosius, one of Constantine's successors, that Christianity followed the example of its erstwhile persecutors and in 395 banned pagan cults. It used to be fashionable to challenge the sincerity of Constantine's conversion, but increasingly historians are accepting it for what he claimed it to be. This may be partly due to the estimates which suggest that Christianity was not as numerically strong as was once thought and so to there being less obvious advantage to Constantine in such a conversion. But probably the principal explanation is simply the willingness of historians to take greater account of the complexities of human motivation at this time. Thus it is entirely compatible with what we know of the period for Constantine to have been motived both by a genuine religious faith and by political ambition and intrigue. In an analogous way in the following century we find St Cyril of Alexandria combining a deep religious conviction with no scruples about resorting even to bribery in order to ensure that the right side won!

Of course even today in many countries bribery is an everyday part of life, and so before we rush to condemn Cyril we would need to ask the same question of the late Roman empire. But rather than pursue that issue, I want to look at the reasons why Constantine chose to delay his baptism until just before his death. To someone unfamiliar with the period it could so easily be read as clear evidence of his lack of commitment to Christianity, whereas once one knows the theological beliefs of the time it can even be used to argue the exact opposite, the strength of his commitment to Christianity. It thus provides a perfect illustration of the need to familiarize oneself with a period before pronouncing on it.

In this case the relevant context was an ongoing Christian debate about the status of post-baptismal sin. The reader can perhaps get nearest to Constantine's mood if he reflects on the way in which even today some recent converts to Christianity can find themselves worrying whether they have perhaps committed the unforgivable sin against the Holy Spirit of which Jesus spoke (Mark 3:29). Since the Holy Spirit is given in baptism and Hebrews 6:4–6 speaks of the impossibility of forgiveness for those who fall away after baptism, the early Church spent much energy debating what sins would constitute such a falling away and these were eventually narrowed down to three: apostasy, adultery and murder. While modern politics may not require the last, the ancient world thought otherwise, and it is into this context too that Constantine's murder of his son and the enforced suicide of his wife should be put. Of course we do not find it easy to set sincere Christian belief against such a backdrop of fear and political intrigue, but unless we make the effort of imagination we will never properly understand the complex character of Christianity's first political patron.

But even if the conversion of Constantine played an integral part in the eventual success of Christianity, it would be folly to suppose his conversion the sole cause. Even if he had been the worst of tyrants, it would have needed other factors to aid its path. Increasing recognition is in fact being given to the higher moral quality of the Christian community as one such element, as for instance in its close pastoral care of its poorer members or in its opposition to infanticide. But one factor that has recently been challenged (by Robin Lane Fox in 1987, in *Pagans and Christians*) is the alleged decline of pagan religion. I mention this for two reasons. Again it illustrates the way in which our prejudices can distort our reading of the evidence: as we saw in chapter 1, pagan religion is not easy to comprehend and from that it is but a short step to supposing that no one has ever taken it seriously. But also, once one has that attitude it is very easy to go on from that to find one's prejudices confirmed by some allegedly salient piece of information, and then leave the matter at that. So in this case a comment from the pagan writer Plutarch about the decline of the famous oracle of Delphi was for long taken as normative, whereas a more rounded look at the evidence has produced a very different picture.

Another factor that may well have played a large role is the development of hierarchical structures within the Church. For this gave an organisational strength to Christianity that paganism lacked, with its absence of sacred books or permanent priesthood (most pagan priests served only for short periods). Catholic scholars used to be concerned to trace the threefold ministry of bishop, priest and deacon back to the New Testament itself but a Roman Catholic like John Meier is now content to admit that dramatic contrasts of organization existed in the early Church. This is one of the fascinations of his joint work with Raymond Brown on *Antioch and Rome* (1983). According to Meier's proposed reconstruction of the history of the church in Antioch (probably the third largest city in the Empire), Matthew's Gospel was written in part to resist any move towards clericalism (cf. 23:1–12), with key decisions taken by the community as a whole (cf. 18:15–20), whereas not much more than fifteen years later the letters of Ignatius assume a church organization with a monarchical bishop at its head. The absence of any reference to predecessors perhaps indicates that Ignatius himself was the first to exercise such a role.

Meier suggests that the reason for the changes in structures was probably either persecution or threat from the heresy of Gnosticism, or perhaps a combination of both. The term 'Gnosticism' comes from the Greek word *gnosis,* which means knowledge. As a religious phenomenon, it took both pagan and Christian forms. But what charactized both was the conviction that knowledge was the way to salvation. Thus in effect knowledge usurped the role played in orthodox Christianity by a personal relationship with Jesus Christ and the ethical demands that brings. The knowlege in question often took rather strange, abstruse forms. But, rather than pursue that matter here, what I want to do is use the way in which our understanding of Gnosticism has developed of late as an effective foil and contrast to Meier's work on Matthew's Gospel.

Different sorts of approach may be required depending on the nature of the evidence. So in the case of Meier it is not that we have any new evidence not previously available, but that this scholar is trying to take seriously other, often overlooked parts of Matthew's Gospel. It is this which explains his rejection of the traditional interpretation of Matthew 16:18: 'Thou art Peter, and upon this rock I will build my church.' For centuries the text has been treated as giving divine sanction to the papacy, with Peter as the first pope. But, despite the fact that he himself is a Roman Catholic, Meier insists that the verse must be read in the light of passages like 18:15–20, where the authority of the whole community is stressed. So he takes this verse as referring symbolically to the entire Church and not just one particular individual (i.e. Peter). By contrast, with Gnosticism it is not a question of reinterpreting the same evidence with new tools (form and redaction criticism) but of there being a vast amount of new data that has emerged from the sands of Egypt. For almost two thousand years we had to rely for our picture of Gnosticism on its portrayal by hostile critics within Christianity, whereas now it can speak for itself, thanks to the discovery of numerous original texts, first at

Oxyrhynchus in 1897 and then at Nag Hammadi in 1947.

The result is that we are now enabled to glimpse something of its attractiveness, but also why it represented such a threat that Christianity could only survive by resisting it. In describing its appeal Hans Jonas in *The Gnostic Religion* (1958) draws parallels with twentieth-century existentialism, while Elaine Pagels in *The Gnostic Gospels* (1979) notes its stress on equality, the status of women and its vision of the knowledge of God as a search for self-knowledge. But its chaotic individualistic pluralism meant that had it successfully infiltrated Christianity it would have become as pluriform as paganism and so just as weak. Instead, the Church united against the threat by strengthening its structures, as well as strengthening its appeal to a written record, two standards against which a shared truth could be measured. So, fairly quickly apart from a few exceptions (Hebrews, Revelation), a common mind was reached on whose perceptions were to be seen as definitive for the Christian faith. Under Constantine a new threat to the identity of Christianity arose in the form of the heresy of Arianism. As a result a third badge of Christian identity came into existence. This was the Nicene Creed, the declaration of belief which is still said today at the Communion Service of most of the major denominations.

The way in which hierarchical structures thus played a key role in bringing about the eventual transformation of Christianity into a world religion provides a salutary lesson. It warns us against assuming naively that biblical norms of thought and practice *necesssarily* suit what may be very different historical circumstances. This is not to challenge the definitive character of the Bible for a Christian account of salvation but it is to remind the reader of my earlier point that it is sometimes necessary to change in order merely to remain the same. New forms of authority had to be introduced if Christian unity was to be preserved across the great expanse of the Roman Empire. A similar question can be raised about Christianity's encounter with pagan philosophy and the infiltration of its language even into the Nicene Creed, as in the phrase that Christ is 'of one substance with the Father'. It is that issue that I will take up next.

Creative transformation through pagan philosophy

This is obviously not the place to go into detail about the sort of philosophy which held sway at this time. It was essentially eclectic in character, predominantly Platonist but with elements drawn from Stoicism. Rather, what is of interest for us to note is the way in which Christianity came (with some reluctance, it must be said) to the recognition that biblical language is not the only way of expressing the Christian faith, and indeed that each generation must seek its own most appropriate way of transmitting what it believes, if it is not to lose touch with the society in which it is set. Some bishops were certainly uneasy when the Greek philosophical phrase 'of the same substance' was introduced into the Nicene Creed of AD 325 in order to define more accurately Christ's relationship with the Father. Perhaps many of my readers would share a similar disquiet over this preference for pagan over biblical terminology, but if so I beg leave to differ.

Christianity had emerged out of what citizens of the Empire would have regarded as one of its less civilized parts, and so if it was to make intellectual headway in the pagan world it had to take seriously the sorts of issues they took seriously. Platonism believed in a wholly transcendent God, a God for whom direct contact with the world was impossible except through intermediaries. In terms of that picture it would have been very easy to have presented Christ as just another intermediary, and everyone would have been happy. But that would have been simply to accommodate oneself to one's culture, not to engage actively in dialogue with it by challenging it. The Church chose the latter, more difficult course because it believed it had something profound to offer the world, the claim that God himself in Jesus had entered into the human condition. But again note that it asserted this in a way that continued the dialogue rather than abandoned it. For it chose to say this in the language of the day that would most clearly assert Christ's divinity, the philosophical language of substance. We ourselves might well choose other language to make the same point (though many pagan philosophers even today still continue to think highly of the precision inherent in such terminology of substance), but even if we did so we should not deny credit to the patristic period for what it attempted to do in its own thought forms. It was simply expressing more clearly what had already been implied by an earlier generation, as in Ignatius' reference to 'Jesus Christ, my God' or in the famous opening verse of St John's Gospel: 'In the beginning was the Word, and the Word was with God, and the Word was God.'

That Prologue of St John in fact provides another interesting illustration of the way in which dialogue enriched understanding. It is now commonly acknowledged that the explanation for John's langugage can be found entirely from within a Palestinian context without reference to the wider Hellenistic world. So what did John mean by 'Word'? We have to think of the way in which rabbinic Judaism meditated on Old Testament references to the 'word' of God. 'In the beginning. . . God said' is how Genesis opens, and in fact throughout the Old Testament 'word' is frequently taken as the symbolic medium through which God acts. 'By the word of the Lord were the heavens made' (Ps. 33:6), we are told, and it is a word that cannot fail to be effective: 'The word is gone out of my mouth in righteousness, and shall not return (unaccomplished)' (Isa. 45:23). So in identifying Jesus with the divine word John is equating him with God's creativity and power.

However, when this Gospel became the property of the wider Church and so was used in dialogue with the philosophy of the time, the words used in this same prologue acquired what seems to me at any rate an altogether richer meaning. When a Greek philosopher wanted to speak of giving an 'account' or 'explanation' of something, the normal Greek word which he would use was *logos*. In other contexts this *logos* could just as easily be translated as 'word', and so it is the expression which St John also uses in his Gospel. The two meanings ('word' and 'explanation') are of course connected in the sense that to give 'word' to an idea in one's mind is to give some 'account' of it. But, however that may be, it was from this latter meaning that it came within philosophy to function like a technical term, meaning something like 'principle of intelligibility or meaning', and that is why in Stoic philosophy the term was written with a capital-letter. For the Stoic claim was that there was an immanent pattern of intelligibility present within the universe and directing it as a whole, and our proper role was to align ourselves with it. The genius of the Church Fathers then consisted in this, in identifying Logos in this Stoic sense with the Logos of John's Gospel but at the same time insisting that such meaning or intelligibility is to be found not by looking to the universe as a whole but rather to the life of one man. For, the argument goes, if one once understands his significance, then one has understood one's own. That is of course a large claim, but it is the claim of traditional Christianity, and more successfully expressed, I believe, by the Church engaging in this way in dialogue with the culture of its time than by turning its back upon it.

Nor should one attempt to confine this problem of trans-lation exclusively to the past. One suspects that most people, when they hear St John's Prologue as the Gospel for Christmas day or at a Carol Service, certainly experience something of the mysterious quality of the Incarnation, but one wonders how much of the content of the claim is conveyed. It may be that once more there is a need to relate it more obviously to the language and thought forms of our own day.

THE MEDIEVAL ACHIEVEMENT

It is quite a jump to move from discussing Christianity in the classical world to a time during which it seemed to exercise complete ascendancy. But here too the possibility of miscon-ception is rife. Depending on prior bias, the reader is probably already disposed to view the medieval period either as an age of tedious, superstitious conformity or as an idyllic time when all of Europe acted and thought as one. The reality was quite otherwise, and so before going on to note a few of the real achievements of the period, I must first attempt to draw back a few of the cobwebs.

Escaping the parody

If one cherishes illusions of the Middle Ages being a totally monolithic society, whether for good or bad, all one need do to disabuse oneself of the idea is read Emmanuel Le Roy Ladurie's fascinating portrayal of the work of the Inquisition in *Montaillou* (1980), a small village in southern France in the early fourteenth century. There was in fact an astonishing range of belief and practice. The thirteenth-century Holy Roman Emperor Frederick II seems to have been an atheist and is alleged to have written a book entitled *Of Three Imposters* in which Moses, Christ and Muhammad were all so branded. But what Le Roy Ladurie's researches have revealed is that such questioning was by no means confined to an educated elite. One instance he quotes is of a peasant who denied both the Resurrection and the Virgin Birth and indeed insisted in the crudest of language that Jesus must have been born of two parents in the usual way.

Of course it was a society in which those in power attempted to control belief, but the extent of that control and its mechanisms can easily be exaggerated. If we continue to take *Montaillou* as our example, what we discover is that the inquisitor concerned, Jacques Fournier, the future Pope Benedict XII, seems to have conducted the proceedings with the best of motives, and in fact to have used torture only once. Indeed, the remarkable thing is that this busy bishop was even willing to spend a fortnight of his valuable time trying to persuade a captive of something as difficult as the truth of the Trinity. So the book is as much a warning against exaggerating the oppressiveness of medieval structures as it is of exaggerating uniformity of belief. Another Frenchman, the distinguished atheist historian of thought, Michel Foucault, can be seen to reinforce this conclusion. Through a series of books he has been concerned to argue that social structures have become more oppressive since the eighteenth century, not less. The treatment of madness, prisoners and sex are among the areas with which he deals. I have not the space to do justice to his arguments here, but essentially his contention is that modern society has developed more effective means of control and so become more oppressive. If we take attitudes to sexuality as our example, it was not until the eleventh century that the Church insisted upon ecclesiastical control of marriage, and even then the ceremony merely took place in the church porch; in fact as late as 866 Pope Nicholas I had declared that mutual consent sufficed even in the absence of all public ceremony, whether civil or religious. The Counter-Reformation's stress on more frequent confession than the once-a-year hitherto required meant a more prurient interest in the details of sexual conduct and, Foucault argues, this was still further accentuated by theories like those of Freud which, so far from liberating, entailed detailed investigation by doctors and educators of areas that had formerly been seen as beyond the range of society's interest. No doubt details of Foucault's thesis can be challenged but its interest lies in the way in which he invites us to reconsider the received view of European history as consistently moving towards a more tolerant society.

Another parody of the period that needs to be questioned is its alleged lack of interest in the Bible. A book by Beryl Smalley on *The Study of the Bible in the Middle Ages* (1964) in fact opens with the remark that 'the Bible was the most studied book of the middle ages'. It was the case that one had to study the Bible for several years before one could go on to study philosophy in the university, and indeed even those who wished to teach philosophy had to begin their teaching career with lectures on the Bible. Of course it is true that there was much ignorance among the ordinary people, but one must remember that this was an age before the invention of printing and so, in part at least, such ignorance could be attributed to economic factors. Certainly serious attempts were made to use the visual medium of stained glass to educate the illiterate majority in the biblical story.

Nor is it true that their approach to Scripture was necessarily inferior to our own. Of course, they lacked all our critical tools, but one immense advantage that (it seems to me) they had over our own culture was the assumption that truth is not always to be found at the literal level. Of course they acknowledged its existence but, following patristic precedent, three further senses were also admitted – the moral, the allegorical and the anagogical or mystical. All have biblical antecedents. For the moral, look for instance at the practical implications drawn from lives of faith in Hebrews 11:1–12:8; for the allegorical, Jesus's own use of the story of Jonah (Matt. 12:39–41); and for the anagogical (the mystical pointing to

heavenly realities), the way in which the author of the Epistle
to the Hebrews interprets the Temple cult as an anticipation of
the sacrifice of Christ.

Of course such an approach often produced rather absurd
results and indeed a total disregard for historical context. But
there were also undoubted advantages. For one thing it meant
that the medieval commentators, like the biblical writers
themselves, took seriously the symbolic meanings behind the
apparently bare historical record. For another, it meant that the
reader's or listener's first priority was always to derive spiritual
lessons from what he read or heard. Bernard, for instance,
heard the Song of Songs not just as a piece of love poetry but
primarily as an expression of Christ's love for his Church. The
book of Joshua, on the other hand, could be read not just as a
bloodthirsty campaign to conquer the Promised Land but also
symbolically as an expression of our own battle to win through
to our own promised land (Heaven) under the leadership of
another and greater Joshua (this being the Hebrew version of
Jesus's name). Indeed, even the total disregard for historical
context by which everyone was portrayed in art in contemporary costume had at least the potential to evoke a lively sense of
their present reality, which of course is precisely the claim that
Christianity would wish to make in any case of Jesus and the
saints in Heaven.

Our debt to the period

I was being deliberately contentious in entitling this section
'the Medieval Achievement': my intention was to provoke the
reader into reconsidering whether the common parodies of the
period are really fair. To justify fully talk of an 'achievement' is
beyond the strictly limited role of an introduction like this. It
would for instance involve us challenging contemptuous
dismissals of scholastic philosophy, which was in fact much
less monochrome than the uninitiated suppose. The rediscovered works of Aristotle engendered a lively debate between
exponents of the new and more empirical approach on the one
hand, and the earlier dominant Platonists on the other; indeed,
such intellectual ferment was occurring in the twelfth century

that many historians choose to speak of a 'twelfth-century renaissance' rivalling the later and more famous Renaissance. But rather than pursue that matter here, I shall instead merely draw the reader's attention to a couple of our more obvious debts to the period, which are still easily available for all to see.

The first is the external appearance of so many of our churches, whether medieval Gothic or in nineteenth-century Gothic copies. In the hustle and bustle of our modern lives very few of us reflect on how profoundly religious an image these churches provide and on how extraordinarily successful it is on its own terms. It is not just a matter of a spire pointing heavenward. In contrast to the earlier Norman or Romanesque style the pillars, the windows and supports are all made as light as possible (compatible with the building staying up) so as to convey this uplifting message. Indeed, considerable structural risks were taken as tall, thin pillars replaced the squat, fat Norman ones and as the stone framework and tracery of the windows was made as slender and delicate as it could be. So the interior just as much as the exterior was designed with this educational objective in view, and throughout the medieval period various experiments in refinement of technique were tried in order to better secure this same underlying objective – the successive modifications of Early English, Decorated and Perpendicular in England, with Flamboyant replacing the last in France and Scotland. However, because churches and cathedrals have often undergone many internal modifications in the course of the centuries, it is perhaps the exterior that makes the most immediate impact. All one need do if one wants to feel its full power is look at a Gothic church on a quiet, moonlit night. Then despite the massiveness of the stone one will be convinced that the whole building is almost about to take off like a rocket!

The continuing influence of the Middle Ages upon us can also be illustrated by asking the question, which of the three elements in Christ's life, his birth, death and resurrection *we* would most choose to emphasize. Some might be inclined to say that all are equally important, but I suspect that nowadays most would opt for the first or second, with the regular church-goer stressing the second and the casual the first, given that Carol Services and Christmas Day are likely to be his main diet of religious observance. Yet if one had asked any Christian prior to the year 1000, almost certainly he would have given pride of place to the Resurrection. Indeed, so central was this that in order to symbolize the event crosses in churches were always left either plain or had a Christ already in majesty upon them, and it was not until shortly before 1000 with the Gero Crucifix in Cologne Cathedral that there first appears our earliest surviving cross with a suffering Christ upon it. Likewise there were no cribs in churches at Christmas until St Francis of Assisi invented the practice in the thirteenth century. For the patristic period it was the *divine* aspect of Christ that was dominant, the God who in his Resurrection had vanquished the powers of evil and so opened up for us new possibilities of life. For the Middle Ages, however, while this image was never denied, there was added to it a tremendous desire for identification with the *human* Christ. It is this which explains not only numerous works of medieval art like the agony portrayed in Grünewald's famous Isenheim Altarpiece but which also contributed to the process which eventually led to our own age's preoccupation with the humanity of Christ.

Against such a background even something as apparently strange as the extensive medieval interest in Jesus's grandparents becomes readily comprehensible. Because the extended family played such a large role it was felt that there would have been something lacking to his full humanity unless there had also been grandparents around to take a similar interest in the growing Jesus. So while the various tales of Joachim and Anna (as they were called) are without historical foundation, it by no means follows that we should therefore dismiss them as no more than mere idle tales. Rather they express in their own unique way medieval society's deep commitment to the humanity of Jesus.

So just as redaction criticism of the Gospels enables us to see that there is more than one way of seeing Jesus, so a study of the Church's history must similarly release us from any thought that there is only one normative way. Indeed, the distinguished church historian Jaroslav Pelikan in his book *Jesus through the Centuries* (1985) lists eighteen!

REFORMATION CONTINUITIES

Once more I have chosen a controversial title in order to encourage the reader to think a bit more deeply about the nature of history. History never occurs in isolation. There is always a context, and that context affects the nature of what happens. So in this instance it would be folly to suppose that the Reformation was just a rejection of the medieval Church; its response was also in part conditioned by the very character of that medieval Church. Equally the way in which Protestant and Catholic approaches developed after the break is a function not just of their different theologies but also of the wider nature of their society as a whole. I shall try to illustrate both contentions in what follows, but before doing so perhaps I should issue two caveats or cautions. First, none of this is to deny the enormous changes that did occur; but the changes are already well-known, the continuities much less so. Secondly, to identify social factors at work is not to belittle the achievement of the Reformers; all of us are subject to these, and all of life involves interaction – us affecting our social environment and it affecting us.

Continuity with the past

As I mentioned earlier in this chapter, one of the great fascinations of historical study is the way in which it forces us to see ourselves in a new light, and one such instance of this is certainly the Reformation. Gone are the days when historians used to present it as a totally new beginning, as simply a return to the purity of the New Testament after all the corruption of the Middle Ages. Instead a much more complex picture is emerging, which requires Protestants to reassess their debt to the medieval Church and Roman Catholics to acknowledge the extent to which the two main Reformers had in fact sought to remain loyal to the essence of the Catholic tradition. Thus on the latter point, though the history of Protestantism turned out very differently, both the main Protestant Reformers, Luther and Calvin, had in fact wished to retain Holy Communion as the main weekly service of the Church. Again, the theology of both Luther and Calvin is dominated by that of a pre-Reformation theologian, St Augustine, who ironically was also the most important theological influence on the individual who was eventually to be declared the pre-eminent theologian of the Roman Catholic Church, namely St Thomas Aquinas. So whether one takes practice or theory there is much more continuity than is commonly appreciated.

On some points the Reformers can sound very 'Catholic' indeed. A good case of this is Luther's attitude to the Eucharist. Because he objected to the doctrine of transubstantiation, it is easy to be misled into supposing that he could not possibly have had as 'high' a view of the reality of Christ's presence in the sacrament as Roman Catholics would wish to claim. But this is refuted by his behaviour at the Colloquy of Marburg in 1529, at which attempts to achieve unity among the Protestant Reformers foundered on Luther's insistence that Jesus's words 'This is my Body' must be interpreted literally. Where he differed from Rome was not in doubting the reality of Christ's physical presence but in thinking it absurdly pretentious of human reason to use Aristotelian metaphysics to show how this could be possible. Again, to take a less central issue but one which might still embarrass most contemporary Protestants, Luther had no hesitation in declaring that any denial of the perpetual virginity of the Virgin Mary would be a gross insult to the one who had had the unique honour of bearing the Incarnate one.

With the illustrations so far given it is a case of reassessing the significance of what is already widely known. But historical scholarship has also disclosed debts that had been forgotten for centuries. This is even true of the most famous doctrine of the Reformation, namely Luther's doctrine of justification by faith. The popular picture is of a medieval Church dominated by a theology of good works as the means of winning favour in God's eyes; Luther then challenges this by insisting that one is justified, that is 'counted as righteous' before God, not by quantity of good works but solely by the faith one puts in God's power to save. Added plausibility could then be given to the picture by referring to Luther's anxieties as a monk about whether his life was really doing all the good

111

that was required of him. Luther's own portrayal of his discovery of justification by faith is certainly that of a happy release from worry, and many since have similarly found comfort in what might otherwise have seemed an impossible task, to show ourselves worthy before God.

Yet the very impossibility of the task ought to have warned us against attributing anything so unlike a gospel or 'good news' to the medieval period, and in fact what scholars have found on investigation is that Luther was reacting against a doctrine of a much more subtle kind, that indeed even today many Protestants, never mind Catholics, might be inclined to accept. To begin with it needs to be emphasized that, whatever popular piety may have thought, certainly at the academic level all theologians were agreed that salvation was primarily a matter of 'grace', that is of God treating us more kindly than we deserve. There was thus certainly never any question of us *deserving* God's esteem. Rather, the nearest theologians ever came to endorsing such a possibility was in the late medieval suggestion that God has entered into a covenant with us to treat certain of our good actions, however inadequate, *as though* they made us worthy to stand in his presence. In much the same way the coins we use today are treated for the purposes of exchange *as though* they are of more worth than the cheap metal from which they are made. Even that much was seen by some medieval theologians as conceding too large a human contribution. But, whether so or not, what the argument makes clear is that Luther's notion of imputed (as distinct from actual) worth already existed in medieval theology. Thus his more limited innovation lay in breaking the connection with any particular good works of ours, not in denying that we could ever *deserve* our salvation, which had never been the medieval claim.

There is not the space here to help the reader arbitrate the issue, but it is important that one should be aware of what precisely is at stake, for that will compel respect for medievalist and Luther alike. The objective of the former was to secure a place for human responsibility, that however much God is seen as always taking the initiative there must be at least some place for human response. Luther saw the difficulty in this, of worrying whether one had ever done what was required of one, however minimal this might be. But the Reformation generated in turn its own difficulty. For faith too came to be seen as wholly a work of God and so nothing whatsoever of the individual's making was seen as guiding the divine choice. It is perhaps hardly surprising that many a later Protestant was to recoil from the doctrine on the grounds that, however much it exalted the divine mercy, it seemed to do so at the cost of any sense of human dignity and worth.

So far in considering the Reformation's continuity with the past, I have confined myself to its ideas. Where practice is concerned, there was little if any continuity. The Mass was abolished, and it is only in modern times that the Protestant churches have returned to more frequent Communion services. Yet there were some senses in which continuity was preserved. As a minor instance which illustrates well the problems of historical interpretation, take the following sentence from Alister McGrath's excellent introduction to *Reformation Thought* (1988): 'The Frenchman Antoine du Prat, Archbishop of Sens, turned up for only one service at his cathedral: his presence and role within this service was somewhat passive, as it was his funeral.' The joke is a good one, and would seem to corroborate well McGrath's point about the general corruption of the medieval church.

Yet, though I know nothing about the individual concerned, it is difficult to argue simply from a bishop's absence from his diocese without indicting the newly formed Protestant churches as well. Queen Elizabeth I, for instance, kept the diocese of Oxford vacant for forty years, but no one would deny her religious sincerity. Again, in the eighteenth century Bishop Richard Watson almost never visited his diocese of Llandaff in Wales. Instead he spent his time in theological writing and in organizing various agricultural inprovements. The point is not that such individuals were corrupt, but that what it was to be a bishop was conceived very differently throughout most of the Church's history from its present purely pastoral conception. Bishops were major political figures in the land and so both State and Church saw their role largely in these terms. Indeed, it is possible to provide even from the late nineteenth century a dramatic instance of this. For Archbishop Tait reprimanded Bishop Samuel Wilberforce for being *too conscientious* in his diocese. It would, he maintained, set a precedent which would make political and national obligations on the part of bishops impossible. Thus, returning to the case of Antoine du Prat, Paris only became an archdiocese in 1622; until that time the Archbishop of Sens was reponsible for the capital, and so it would scarcely be surprising if most or all of his time were devoted to supporting the interests of the Church at the royal court.

So what would be taken by us as an indubitable sign of corruption need not be seen so in terms of the context of the times. But this is by no means an isolated case of where a fresh look at the facts can lead to a reassessment of the nature of continuities at this time. As a result there is now much greater readiness among historians to challenge the view that the Reformation was everywhere welcomed as a release from the corruptions of the medieval Church. Thus, if we confine ourselves to England, while the previous generation of British historians like A. G. Dickens and G. R. Elton had seen the Reformation as popular and inevitable, more recent writing has tended to stress its contingent character. England could easily have remained Catholic, given just a slightly different set of circumstances. An obvious example of this new approach is J. J. Scarisbrick's *The Reformation and the English People* (1984) which presents a wealth of information to suggest that Catholic piety was in fact flourishing in England on the eve of the Reformation. For instance, the evidence from surviving wills indicates great generosity to ecclesiastical causes, while such factors as the gradual character of the dissolution of the monasteries, the fact that people had to be paid for removing Catholic symbols from churches, or the ease with which they could be restored again in the reign of Mary, all would seem to unite in indicating a nation unenthusiastic for change. Perhaps the truth will eventually be seen as lying somewhere in between, but certainly it is no longer possible to paint the story in the simplistic colours of the past, of a Church hopelessly corrupt whose reform was eagerly endorsed by the majority.

As one last example that illustrates well both the problem of interpreting the facts and this question of continuity, let me take the issue of clerical celibacy. A former generation took the high number of investigations of clerical misconduct as indicative of a rule more honoured in the breach than in the observance, whereas today many scholars are prepared to argue that the very fact of action being thought worth while must indicate general observance. The result is that some estimates now suggest that as much as between 80 and 90 per cent of the clergy in Europe were conforming to the rules. However that may be, attitudes by no means changed immediately. Elizabeth, the third English Protestant monarch, strongly disapproved of clerical marriage and even went so far as to address the wife of one Archbishop of Canterbury, Matthew Parker, in the following terms: 'Madam, I may not call you; mistress, I'm ashamed to call you; and so I know not what to call you; but, howsoever, I thank you.'

Geneva and Rome marching in step

Calvin's Geneva, symbol of Protestantism and Rome, symbol of Catholicism marching in step! That is quite a claim. I do not want, of course, to deny the enormous differences between the Protestant and Roman Catholic reaction once the Reformation had occurred. But in order to get the reader to think a bit more deeply about the nature of historical development, let me draw attention to some of the *similarities* of reaction, which may be less well known.

The first and most obvious point of similarity is that the sixteenth century in fact produced not one Reformation, but two: for corresponding to the Protestant Reformation was the Catholic Counter-Reformation. The Counter-Reformation not only corrected the undoubted abuses which existed; it also launched major new religious orders like the Jesuits who were to play such a large missionary role on the American continent and in the Far East. It created new forms of piety as in the Spanish mystics, Teresa of Avila and John of the Cross, and produced major social reformers like Charles Borromeo and Francis de Sales; it also gave impetus to an important new form of religious art, the Baroque.

115

But of late what has interested historians is less the reforms themselves and more the extent to which, despite the very different forms they took, both movements were influenced by the underlying social trend towards increasing individualism. This stemmed intellectually from the Renaissance as well as materially from the increased power of the middle classes. John Bossy ends his *Christianity in the West 1400–1700* (1985) with the comment that by the seventeenth century the very word 'Christianity' had changed its meaning from a body of people to a body of beliefs – something *one* person could hold – and this privatization of religion he sees as something that affected Counter-Reformation as much as Reformation. That is to say, both experienced the turn towards a much more individualistic understanding of religion and in this respect at least have more parallels than differences.

Thus, for example, rather than seeing baptism as one's badge of social membership of the community, both now stressed the need for instruction in the faith, though with this difference: that while Protestantism stressed the Ten Commandments, Rome laid emphasis on the Creed. Again, not only did both accept the introduction of the pew which tended to highlight social divisions, both stressed forms of training that made access more difficult for humbler members of society. Thus Protestantism's stress on the sermon must have made it more difficult for the less intellectual members of a congregation to absorb what was said as their own, and indeed this problem must have been considerably exacerbated by the increased learning of the clergy. No longer the local boy not much more educated than themselves, the minister was now well-read and university educated. But there was a similar problem generated on the Catholic side through new attitudes to confession. It was now seen very much in terms of an interior monitoring and training of the soul and, as such, very frequent confession was required, in contrast to the once-a-year stipulated by the Fourth Lateran Council in 1215. For this to be properly effective it required regular access to a continuing spiritual director, and inevitably this was easier for the well-to-do. The introduction of the confessional box still further privatized the conception of the act. One was no longer doing what was simply required of one as a member of society. One was acting as an individual to restore one's personal relationship with God. The result was that as with Protestantism, it was no longer easy for the nominal Catholic to enter into the spirit of his Church because the act he chose to perform occasionally only made sense to the pious Catholic in terms of a regular, developing pattern of behaviour. The result of this was that both versions of Christianity equally experienced difficulty in communicating to some sectors of society.

Sometimes the apparently insignificant is the best guide to an age, and in this case changed attitudes to communal eating are a good case in point. In the Middle Ages there had been no forks and knives but everyone had used their fingers to help themselves out of communal bowls. In the days before a proper understanding of hygiene the introduction of separate bowl and utensils had probably more to do with this increasing sense of individualism. But in any case it is interesting to note that even as late as 1573 Veronese had a painting of his condemned on the grounds that he had depicted one of the Apostles at the Last Supper using a fork. The objection was not of course one of historical accuracy. Rather it was a question of what it meant to be a Christian community: an interdependent whole (as in the medieval model) or a group of independently acting individuals (as in the more modern view).

Ironically, this move away from a social understanding of religion to a more individualistic pattern is now being used to explain one of the most extraordinary aspects of post-Reformation England. Nearly all the executions for witchcraft in England occurred in the latter part of the sixteenth century and the first three-quarters of the seventeenth century. Medieval England had believed in witches, but they were pursued with nothing like the same venom, a venom that was reflected in various Acts of Parliament, the last of which was not repealed until 1736. Keith Thomas's *Religion and the Decline of Magic* (1975) provides the explanation that with the removal of the supportive framework of saints and guardian angels and the increased stress on individual responsibility this produced an age of anxiety in which the Devil came increasingly to be seen as a suitable scapegoat to blame for one's own failures. Many accusations seem to have been induced by failure in one's social obligations. So, for instance, if one did not help some old woman at the door and something subsequently went wrong in the household, rather than facing the guilt the tendency was to blame the old woman for her spells instead.

But perhaps this individualistic emphasis is seen most prominently in the principal doctrine of the Reformation to which we have already referred, justification by faith. Although the stress is very much on what God has done (that is, declared the individual righteous in God's eyes by virtue of what God himself has done on the Cross), its effect was highly individualistic, since the benefits were only appropriated by the individual having faith that this was indeed so. It may be thought that the medieval idea of acquiring merit in God's eyes through works of goodness (however qualified, as we have seen) is equally individualistic. But it needs to be recalled that these were viewed in terms of a wider 'treasury of merit', so that one could intend one's good acts for the benefit of another, for example a member of one's family or a friend in purgatory. It is this doctrine which gave the sale of indulgences their justification, the very issue that sparked off Luther's first protest in 1517. When Rome gave its final definitive reply at the Council of Trent it was with a decree that firmly stressed individual responsibility in the context of a divine graceful justification of the individual. So intellectually, as well as in the practices to which I have referred, we have here our own age dawning with all its stress on the individual, both for good and for bad.

4

The Continuing Task

In each of the chapters so far the reader has been presented with what may well have been seen as a bewildering, if fascinating, variety of approaches to religious questions. This is in itself not surprising. There would have been very much the same result had we taken the history of art or morality. But no adequate discussion can leave the matter there. Just as there are values that we want to propagate today in art and morality, so most people in the world still have some sort of religious sensibility, however vague. We could of course stop there, and treat our own experience as normative, in no way to be challenged, but that would go against everything we have said in this book so far. All our thinking is influenced by the society in which we live and so we must avoid the pretence that our own age is innately superior, whereas in fact it will have its own characteristic prejudices like any other.

Of course it is not easy to see ourselves as others would have seen us, but that is one advantage of the sort of studies discussed in previous chapters. It enables us to appreciate better some of the criticisms that might be levelled against our own culture. Thus to the ancient world with all its stress on myth and the symbolic role of language our own age must seem absurdly literalistic with its constant stress on facts rather than meaning and significance. Our tendency is to treat rich and allusive biblical metaphors and images as though they were intended as strictly defined doctrines. Again, our chapter on 'The Bible's Theologians' revealed a community very much on the move. Though respectful of the past, it did not hesitate to endorse very major changes in its understanding of that past, as it felt it came to know better God's will for the present and future. Yet many contemporary Christians display an almost paranoid fear of all change. Similarly, those aspects of the history of the Church discussed in chapter 3 contain their own implicit critique of our present attitudes and practices. Think, for instance, of the willingness of the Church to engage seriously with pagan culture during the patristic period, or the very strong sense of communal identity and interdependence which existed during the Middle Ages, or the enthusiastic search for the heart of the gospel by both Reformation and Counter-Reformation during a period of crisis in the life of the Church. So in considering what we want to say theologically today, we would be well advised to do so at least in part in dialogue with this past.

But of course it is also true that in many ways our own age has its own unique problems and challenges. Most of these have their origin in the nineteenth century, but have only really come to full expression in the twentieth. For instance, David Friedrich Strauss's *Life of Jesus* of 1836 shattered the faith of many who had a very literalistic understanding of the Bible, including his translator, the novelist George Eliot. But, as we saw in chapter 2, biblical criticism, in the shape of form and redaction criticism, are in fact twentieth-century developments, and these have had as yet no impact on ordinary church life, not even in sermons. Again, though the social sciences date their origin to the nineteenth century, it is only really in the twentieth that they have come to be used as a commonplace objection to the objectivity of religion.

In so short a compass I can only deal with a very few areas of current debate. What I have chosen to do, therefore, is to devote the second part of this chapter to two objectives. First I shall attempt to illustrate a general disagreement within theology about what its starting point should be, whether appeal to general human experience or to revelation; then I plan to discuss three specific areas of current debate, and here my aim will be to identify some of the principal types of argument used within contemporary theology. But before proceeding to these tasks I ought to say something about what many readers may regard as the most fundamental issue of all, namely whether there is sufficient justification for even speaking of God in the modern world.

The current debate

The rationality of religious belief is usually seen as an issue within the philosophy of religion. In subsequent sections we will explore the reasons that have led many theologians to view this whole discussion as either totally misconceived or, at any rate, too narrowly confined. But let me first characterize the nature of the debate, as it currently exists within the Anglo-American, analytic tradition of philosophy. One may usefully distinguish two camps. On the one hand there are those like Richard Swinburne (for God's existence) and J. L. Mackie (against), who identify the heart of the issue as lying in whether proofs of God's existence can be offered. On the other, there are those like D. Z. Phillips and Alvin Plantinga who think that the character of religious belief is such as to make any request for such proofs inappropriate.

Of those two camps it is the former which is closer to the way in which discussion has been conducted in the past. But there are important differences which need to be noted. In chapter 1 we have already encountered one of the traditional arguments for God's existence, the cosmological. In the past each of these arguments was interpreted deductively. That is, the conclusion was seen as following strictly from the premises as in this commonly used illustration of a deductively valid argument: All men are mortal. Socrates is a man. Therefore Socrates is mortal. The point about such arguments is that they either offer strict proof that cannot be challenged, or they show nothing at all. Many famous philosophers of the past have thought that such deductive proofs of God's existence were possible. Numbered among them are St Thomas Aquinas, the most famous philosopher of the Middle Ages, and René Descartes, the early seventeenth-century French thinker who is often regarded as the founder of modern philosophy. But in the eighteenth century such 'proofs' became subject to very severe criticism from the Scottish philosopher, David Hume, and the German, Immanuel Kant. As a result the confidence of philosophers to give conclusive proofs of God's existence waned.

It is against this background that the current discussion should be seen. What Richard Swinburne proposes is that arguments for God's existence should be interpreted *inductively* rather than deductively. That is, his suggestion is that we treat them (on the model of scientific reasoning) as cumulative towards a conclusion that is more probable than not, rather than as demonstrating deductively what must be the case (as in strict mathematical proof). All of us in fact use such inductive arguments in our everyday lives, whenever we attempt to generalize from our experience. For instance, all the swans we have seen so far in life are white; so we conclude that all swans are white. But that must remain only a *probable* conclusion, since we have by no means inspected all the swans in existence. Swinburne presents his case with considerable philosophical rigour and so his discussion is not easily accessible to the philosophically uninitiated, but certainly this is the way the arguments are likely to go if they are to be retained as formal arguments, though there are still a few philosophers who write as though Hume and Kant never existed.

But one should be aware that this is only one approach, and that both in Britain and in the United States many philosophers deny the need for theology to give any justifying reasons for its existence at all. The Welsh philosopher D. Z. Phillips argues that religion can only be understood in terms of its own internal practices and their rules, and so the very request for a justification is seen as a mistake. Meanwhile the American, Alvin Plantinga, maintains that for the religious believer his belief functions something like a 'basic belief' and because of that it makes no sense to ask him to justify his belief in terms of something still more basic, shared by believer and non-believer alike. Put so starkly, neither position may sound very plausible, but each is backed by an impressive appeal to wider considerations.

In the case of Phillips reference is made to this century's most famous philosopher, Ludwig Wittgenstein, and his notion of 'language games', the way in which words can only be properly understood in the context of their use. If that is so, the argument goes, it is simply a mistake to extract a word like 'God' out of the context of worship and religious practice where it has its natural home and move it into the very different framework of philosophical argument. For such a transition entails that the same meaning cannot be maintained throughout for central terms like 'God'. Phillips makes his point by parodying Psalm 139: If I ascend up into heaven, is it the case that thou art there? if I make my bed in hell, is it the case that thou art there? (contrast Ps. 139:8). To address someone in trust (as in the original version) is hardly the same thing as to address him as a question mark!

In the case of Plantinga the appeal instead is to all the doubts which have been raised in the twentieth century about the sort of rationality (called foundationalism) which Descartes as the founder of modern philosophy left to his successors. Descartes built up his philosophy from what we can know for certain. His famous *cogito, ergo sum* (I think, therefore I am), for instance, established the indubitability of the *cogito* from the fact that even in doubting that I think, I am thinking. What Plantinga does is challenge the assumption that the commonly held foundations of knowledge (and thus what may be built on these foundations) are obvious at all. Perhaps a parallel will help. Once upon a time philosophers used to think that we knew only our own existence for certain and that the existence of others was something inferred from our own, and so less 'basic'. But the problem with such a claim is that so much of our self-understanding is heavily dependent upon others. For instance, in order to express our thoughts we need others to teach us language. So it is far from clear what is more 'basic' than what, in this context. Similar problems, Plantinga argues, are encountered with religious belief. Initially it may seem that belief in God is merely something added by the believer to other, more basic beliefs that he has and which he shares with non-believers. But one's religious beliefs affect one's view of the world. For instance, the believer points to the beauty of creation where the atheist may see only the workings of the laws of nature. In short, believer and non-believer view the world (and not only God) in different ways, and so, Plantinga aruges, it is far from clear what should rightly be seen as more basic. But, if that is so, why should the religious believer be required to justify his belief in God in terms of something only allegedly more basic?

Part of the fascination of the philosophy of religion is simply looking at this range of considerations in detail, and assessing their plausibility. But I am conscious that a forbidding degree of technicality may already have been introduced. So, rather than pursue the debate, let me attempt to give it a wider context and one which should be more readily accessible.

A wider context

Frequently one finds that many a believer and non-believer are operating with a very simple, almost naive view of how we know things. It is thought that it must all be a matter of proof or all a matter of faith. It is in fact very easy to get bewitched into thinking that only *conclusive* demonstration is of any value, but very little of life is like that. Take for instance the 'proof' offered by the prosecution in a murder case. What is meant is something like the most plausible interpretation of the evidence, not that no conceivable doubt could still exist. After all, it does happen that as a result of such · 'proof' sometimes someone who subsequently turns out to have been innocent has been executed. Again, most scientists would want to claim that the various sub-atomic particles which have been postulated in recent years are the best way of interpreting the data so far, but, though they believe in them, they would not want to suggest that they have absolutely conclusive reasons for doing so. In fact there is a large amount of literature in the philosophy of science which questions whether science can strictly be seen as advancing all the time by evidence at all. Instead, suggested Thomas Kuhn in *The Structure of Scientific Revolutions* (1962), major advances occur by revolutions in interpretative frameworks rather than by new empirical discoveries. Someone like Newton or Einstein developed an *intuition*, which suggested a better framework for understanding, though almost everything was in fact still capable of explanantion under the old model. Again, if you look at the companion volume to this present book, *Invitation to Philosophy* by Martin Hollis, you will discover that even modern atheist philosophers like W. v. O. Quine no longer exhibit the old certainties about the power of reason. Instead, Quine sees our beliefs as more like a spider's web. It then becomes a matter of how close to the edge of that web one puts a particular belief which determines how easily it will fall off the edge, and that will vary from community to community and from person to person. As Quine puts it in his own inimitable way, Homer's gods and physical objects on this view differ only in degree and not in kind. It depends where people have put them on their web. In other words, one must disabuse oneself of the idea that there are any easy knock-down arguments where conceptual systems clash, and this is a general feature of a certain level of abstract thinking and not just peculiar to theology. Indeed, when one realizes how quickly one reaches an impasse when discussing practical issues such as abortion because of the different conceptual presuppositions involved, it is surprising how anyone could ever have thought otherwise.

But equally this does not mean that we should jump to the opposite extreme and think reasons irrelevant to belief. Though they will not prove beyond all doubt the rightness of the religious case, they can be used to make it more intelligible or plausible, or indeed the reverse. The most obvious case of the latter is the fact of evil in the world. As a deductive, conclusive argument against God's existence it just does not work, for there is no necessary contradiction between asserting God's goodness and omnipotence and admitting the presence of such evil in the world. Even omnipotent goodness cannot bring about what is logically impossible, and there would seem to be no way of guaranteeing simultaneously truly free and truly good human beings. Freedom implies that ability to do otherwise, and so even God could not guarantee that we would always do the good, unless he abrogated our freedom. But that of course does not mean that the fact of evil has ceased to count against God's existence, only that it has ceased to count conclusively. So the believer has still to try to make sense of evil, to show that it can have a meaning, if the atheist is not to be seen as having very strong reasons against religious belief.

But not all of these reasons can easily be put in terms of formal arguments, and that is why it seems to me to be a mistake to assume that analytic philosophy of religion can offer us the whole picture concerning the reasonableness or otherwise of religious belief. Think, for example, of the way in which Dostoevsky conducts his discussion of the problem of evil in *The Brothers Karamazov*. On the one hand he concedes the awfulness of the suffering of innocent children which he cannot explain, but on the other he refuses to let this shake his belief in God since, as he tries to illustrate through the novel in the lives of Mitya, Aloysha and Zosima, he does detect divine grace at work, working in us despite ourselves. So in the end he decides to take more seriously the one rather than the other. Nor is this unreasonable or dogmatic. Indeed it may well be the non-believer who is the more dogmatic. For the Christian at least admits that certain forms of suffering count against his belief in God, whereas the atheist may well insist in giving a reductionist account of these cases of grace, of God creatively at work to bring good out of suffering. It is all psychologically induced, he may say. But in insisting on such an account instead of admitting in turn that these may count against his own views, who is in the end being the more dogmatic? So the believer should certainly not allow himself to be forced into the corner of pronouncing his own beliefs irrational.

But of course the problem is deeper than this. For part of the difficulty is that believer and non-believer do not even see the pain and the good that can emerge from it in the same way. Without suffering there could be no sympathy, nothing towards which to show compassion. Again, without something evil to be afraid of there could be no such thing as courage in facing up to it. To the believer the world is a better place because it allows the existence of virtues like these and the free choice whether to pursue or reject them, whereas all the atheist sees in the situation is the pain which makes such virtues possible. Thus in the end one is faced with two very different frameworks for viewing the world. For the Christian pain is capable of being given a meaning by God entering into the situation as he did with Jesus on the Cross, and transforming it. Even the centurion in charge of the soldiers crucifying him came to see the world in a new light (Mark 15:39), as did the penitent thief hanging by his side (Luke 23: 40–3). That is why for the Christian the Resurrection does not just witness to the fact that Jesus is still alive today but also serves as a symbol of the way in which new life can be brought out of even the most wretched of conditions by God's aid.

In short, religious belief is a decision to read the world in a particular way by valuing certain things rather than others, but that no more makes it irrational than the atheist's choosing to highlight other features of the world instead. One can only think this for so long as one thinks of God as an optional extra, possibly to be added to what is so far a purely neutral reading of the world. But, as I have tried to indicate, there is no such neutral reading. Perhaps the reason why even believers sometimes think in this way is because we are actually in some ways less sophisticated than the myth-makers of chapter 1. For they saw all the world imbued with the divine, whereas many of us seem to think in terms of a God out there who only now and again pops into our world to do something, or perhaps not even that much. The picture then becomes that of a God who, having created the world, then just leaves us to get on with it. Small wonder that in such a context even the devout Christian can be persuaded into supposing that God is just something added to an agreed corpus of ordinary beliefs about the world, rather than something that affords the profound possibility of bringing about their creative transformation.

CONFLICT IN METHOD

But even with God's existence granted, the theologian's problems in attempting to speak to the modern world are by no means at an end. For the student new to this area soon finds that there is no agreed methodology about where one should begin. In this it is by no means unique among arts subjects. Philosophy, for instance, divides into the analytic or continental approach (depending on whether one starts with the analysis of language or reflection on experience), psychology into Freudian and Jungian schools and many more, and so on. Within theology probably the most basic divide of all is that between those who think that theology should have its foundations in the nature of the world as a whole and our experience of it and those who think that theology must start from some given, either the Bible or the Church. Typical representatives of the former would be Paul Tillich (d. 1965) and Karl Rahner (d. 1984) and of the latter Karl Barth (d. 1968) and Hans Urs von Balthasar (d. 1988). The fact that I have mentioned one Protestant and one Roman Catholic in each case shows that the issue is not necessarily an ecclesiastical divide.

What is at stake in fact is how God communicates with the world. Clearly no one could call him or herself a Christian and ignore the Bible and Church. For Christ is the heart of the Christian faith and while the Bible contains the record of his life, we can only appreciate its significance as it has been communicated and preserved in the life of the Church. So the issue is rather how much or how little of God is known apart from that context. Tillich detected in everyone a religious impulse towards worship, though in our own secular society it takes the form of false gods like money, sex or power. So he saw it as the major task of theology to demonstrate the inadequacy of these 'objects of ultimate concern' and to point to where this ultimate concern properly lay. Similarly Rahner suggested that we all, believer and non-believer alike, experience various signs of transcendence in our lives and that when people properly respond to these they are already in a sense 'anonymous Christians'. By contrast Barth argued that ordinary human perceptions are so badly off-target that it is only by God breaking through them and overthrowing them that there is any hope of the truth emerging at all. That is why for Barth the Bible is all-important as the revelation of a God who inverts human pretensions and values. In a similar way Balthasar sees religious understanding emerging not out of the everyday experience of human beings but from those who have responded to a divine call to conversion, transformation and holiness.

Dangers are present in both types of approach, or perhaps

one should say the same danger, since the problem arises at precisely the same point, when the theologian concerned, having fully characterized his starting-point, then goes on to say something about what lies outside that starting-point. Tillich in fact ended up treating the Bible as not essentially different from his own reflections. It became a mythic system in which it did not matter whether Jesus had existed as an historical person. Meanwhile Barth (particularly in his early works) reads as though no good could ever come out of human culture, which makes it puzzling why we should think of the world as a divine creation at all. The truth, it seems to me, must lie somewhere in between. But rather than argue for that here, let me instead draw attention to some of the implications of the two types of method, and in particular how both have their origins in nineteenth-century theology.

Appeal to experience

The eighteenth century was quintessentially the Age of Reason. Never perhaps in the history of man had confidence in the power of human reason been stronger, and so it was perhaps not surprising that such an age of confidence (the 'Enlightenment'), while not denying the existence of God, should be happy to assume that God, having created us, was now content to trust us to our own resources without further divine interference. One way in which this confidence expressed itself was in the French Revolution of 1789. Some confiscated churches were actually dedicated to the cult of Reason. But the speed with which that Revolution degenerated into Robespierre's Reign of Terror,and the subsequent dictatorship of Napoleon, were two of the many factors that contributed to the reaction in European society that we now know as the Romantic Movement. With its stress on feeling and experience rather than reason, this reached its peak in the early part of the nineteenth century. Readers familiar with the poems of William Wordsworth or the novels of Sir Walter Scott will already be aware of something of its character.

It is into this context that two of the great nineteenth-century religious thinkers, Schleiermacher and Hegel, should be set. In contrast to writers of the previous century both insisted upon the immanence of God, on his presence in, and involvement with, every aspect of the world. Hegel saw the history of the world as, in a sense, God's history, as a reflection of his experience of it, in which we participate. Schleiermacher, on the other hand, sought to identify the source of religion in the way in which all human beings experience their existence as radically contingent (as what might not have been). They experience themselves as ultimately dependent on something other than themselves, though of course they may not necessarily identify the object of that feeling with anything resembling the Christian God.

Schleiermacher is often called the father of modern theology. This is certainly true in the sense that many twentieth-century theologians, including Tillich and Rahner, make appeal to experience central to theology in much the same way as Schleiermacher once did with his reference to feelings of 'absolute dependence'. Of the two, Tillich is certainly the easier to read without help. So I shall take Rahner as my example here. Like Schleiermacher he wants to say that there are pointers to God in all our experience, not just when it is explicitly religious. One analogy sometimes used is of God being everywhere about us like light. Just as without light, though we are normally unconscious of it, it would be impossible to see physical objects, so with the ubiquitous presence of God. Rahner's argument is that, though we are normally unaware of it, without it there would be none of those experiences which draw us out of ourselves and cause us to give a worth to human existence that is not reducible to the physical or natural plane. Our moral experience is one case in point. For when we give an infinite worth to human beings, this worth is beyond any actual or potential worth the individual may have to the society in which they are set. This infinite valuing can be read as God drawing us to a recognition of the worth *he* has assigned to us by making us personal like himself.

One should not suppose these experiences to be narrowly confined to those which have an immediate and obvious connection with religion. For instance, the Tantric movement within Hinduism has for centuries been arguing that sexual union is one of the clearest intimations of the divine, because in union with the other the sense of time is suspended and self-identity is lost. Christianity has always treated such images with great caution, but there is surely something odd about our culture when we have to make sacred what previous generations would have already regarded as such. Thus with the decline of saying grace before meals, food and drink have ceased to be seen as gifts and so the Eucharist becomes an isolated act of making secular things sacred rather than giving deeper meaning to what are already active symbols of the sacramentality of the entire universe, which can everywhere be experienced as a pure gift of beauty and joy. The sociologist Peter Berger's book *A Rumour of Angels* (1970) is particularly good at forcing us to think more widely about how intimations of the supernatural are innate to our experience. As well as hope and order he also mentions play for much the same reason as the Indian mystics stressed sex. For one need only watch children at play to notice the way in which time becomes suspended, so totally absorbed are they in what they are doing. Again he chooses to mention what may seem a scarcely less likely candidate, namely humour. But the power of humour to deflate even the most powerful or awful of human institutions, as for instance with Charlie Chaplin's portrayal of Hitler in *The Great Dictator*, cannot help raising for some the question of whether beyond all such relativizations there is not something that cannot be ralativized, something which, though we may laugh at that too, still transcends any limits that we try to impose with our humour. Of course none of this proves the existence of God, but then that is not the point. The point is to indicate a context in terms of which a belief in a divine source of value immanently at work in the world can seem entirely reasonable, if not proven.

Stress on revelation

If Schleiermacher and Hegel were the two major figures of the nineteenth century responsible for producing one kind of theological thinking, Kierkegaard was the most important in producing the other, and in fact both Barth and Balthasar are generous in acknowledging their debt to him. What particularly worried Kierkegaard was the extent to which the Danish Church of his time was totally conformist. It in no way stood out from the society in which it was set and offered no critique of it, and he blamed Hegelian influence as in part responsible for this. Whether this was fair to Hegel we need not discuss here. What we can say is that Kierkegaard successfully identified the inherent danger in all such appeals to experience, that the biblical record is seen as only confirming that experience rather than as issuing radical challenges to it. Yet if the heart of the Christian gospel is that God had intervened in human history by becoming man, this surely must mean that the event must have something of decisive and distinctive importance to say to humanity.

The theology of the Danish church is Lutheran, and it is certainly at Luther's door that part of the blame for its nineteenth-century stagnation must be put. This was perhaps the inevitable result of his doctrine of two kingdoms with its sharp distinction between two separate areas of life, the religious and the social, and its consequent privatization of the former. It was a doctrine which was to have even more tragic consequences in the twentieth century with the failure of the Lutheran church to resist the rise of Nazism. But ironically it is also of course to Luther that one can trace Kierkegaard's interpretation of the gospel as a challenge to radical change and conversion. Indeed, one major factor in turning Luther from monk and university professor into protesting reformer was learning of Erasmus's discovery that the opening words of Jesus's ministry in Matthew 4:17 were not just a demand to do one's social duty and make amends (the Latin read 'do penance') but a call for radical conversion (the Greek is 'repent', which implies a complete change of mental direction).

If Kierkegaard's theology was worked out in reaction against the church of his day in his native Denmark, Karl Barth's was worked out in reaction to the conduct of the church in Germany. The professors who had taught him had schooled him in the theology of Schleiermacher, and it was shock at the ease with which they all supported the Kaiser's declaration of war in 1914 which led him to begin to seek out an alternative theological method. It was a conviction which was then reinforced by the fact that only a minority of the clergy supported the famous Barmen Declaration of 1934 expressing opposition to Hitler, and for which he was deprived of his chair at Bonn and forced to return to his native Switzerland. No doubt this past history of the Church in Germany does much to explain the heavy involvement in politics of her best-known living Protestant theologian, Jürgen Moltmann.

This is not of course to say that it is only a belief in revelation as theology's proper starting point that can generate strong political commitment. Tillich found himself expelled from his chair in Frankfurt by the Nazis even sooner than Barth, in 1933, and he was to spend the rest of his life in exile from his native land, in the United States. But in the case of Moltmann it is not just his political perspective that he believes to have been transformed by revelation, but his conception of God as well. His best-known book is called *The Crucified God* (1974) and in that he is concerned to argue that theology has been dominated too long by philosophical considerations which hold that God cannot suffer without compromising his divinity. On this view it is, strictly speaking, only the humanity of Jesus which suffers on the Cross, not his divinity. The argument is that since God is the source of all and thus not dependent on anything he cannot be affected by something so obviously other than himself, like suffering. But, Moltmann argues in reply, though our natural intuitions may thus argue for God's complete independence from the world as its source, the Bible has overthrown these intuitions by revealing a very different sort of God, deeply involved in human suffering even to the extent of crucifixion.

There is thus no doubt that this question of methodology does raise real and important questions. This is not the place for me to attempt to resolve the issue. Rather, just as I have drawn attention to some of the limitations of beginning with an appeal to experience, let me end this section by noting that stress on revelation is also not without its difficulties. An obvious problem is that, the more one exalts the contribution revelation makes, the greater is the temptation to demote the human contribution, which then reinforces the reasons why we need the divine contribution so much. But not only does this demean the dignity of human beings, it demeans God himself as the creator of our capacity to reflect on our experience of his activity in the world. This was certainly a fault at the Reformation and one from which Barth himself was not entirely free.

It is no doubt for this reason that some contemporary theologians sympathetic to this approach now express themselves more cautiously in terms of the biblical perspective *correcting* rather than necessarily overthrowing our existing assumptions. This is very much better, but one still wonders whether there is sufficient acknowledgement of the extent to which, just as in previous ages, there has to be a dynamic interaction between the Bible and our culture before the Bible can speak clearly. Gone are the days when, with Calvin, it might be possible to talk of the Scriptures as written by 'secretaries of the Holy Spirit' and so as always directly expressing in every sentence the divine will for every age. Instead chapter 2 disclosed a much more complicated picture of biblical composition, with the biblical writers freely adapting the past to speak to the present, a pattern which we saw continued in the subsequent history of the Church. Yet believing Christians today are surprisingly reluctant to take this lesson to heart. Both Roman Catholic and Protestant theologians alike seem content to jump straight from the Bible to the twentieth century. Yet what that ignores is the lesson of the past that the Church has been most successful when it has been most actively engaged in dialogue with the culture in which it happens to find itself.

Another great theologian of the nineteenth century, John Henry Newman, had no difficulty in accepting this fact. When Darwin's *Origin of Species* appeared in 1859, so natural did Newman find the Church's need to adapt to changed circumstances that, unlike so many of his contemporaries, he admitted that he had no difficulty in 'going the whole hog with Darwin'. Not only did he see truth sometimes emerging only gradually over centuries, he realized that sometimes Christianity had to change dramatically in order to remain the same, as in its translation into Greek ways of thinking during the patristic period. Indeed, in one of his most famous statements he even went so far as to say: 'In a higher world it is otherwise; but here below to live is to change, and to be perfect is to have changed often.'

But enough has probably now been said about general questions of method. So I shall end by taking three specific areas where change has been advocated to illustrate the nature of theological argument today.

THEOLOGICAL ARGUMENT

The three areas I have chosen to exemplify some of the most common considerations brought to play in contemporary theology are all aspects of the subject still very much under discussion and all with very definite practical implications. So almost certainly the reader new to theology will find the rest of this chapter very much easier to follow. The topics concerned are Liberation theology, feminist theology and the liturgical movement. What makes the choice especially interesting is the fact that the impetus for change has been rather different in each case-in Liberation theology in large part from a recovery of the meaning of the Old Testament, in feminist theology from a critique of the Church by secular culture, and in the liturgical movement from a realization of how far the practice of all the denominations had diverged from the worship of the primitive Church.

Liberation theology

Liberation theology is in fact little more than twenty years old, for the origins of the movement can be dated to a meeting of Latin-American bishops at Medellin in Mexico in 1968, though the first major work, Gustavo Gutierrez's *A Theology of Liberation*, did not appear until three years later. The term 'Liberation theology' represents the sub-continent's search for self-respect and its dislike of the once popular notion of 'development', which was taken to suggest something that the developed world does to other nations, rather than something that people can do for themselves. In other words, what was being objected to was the notion of a 'solution' imposed from without, particularly since this was often taken to mean an increase in the nation's wealth without any corresponding benefit to the great mass of the people, especially those living in the poverty of the countryside and in the shanty towns which have sprung up all around Latin-American cities. But that would only be to tell half the tale and to omit the religious dimension at that.

One problem with a religion as old as Christianity is that what were once powerful metaphors have lost their original force and meaning. This is true of 'salvation' and 'redemption' which, if they mean anything at all to the unchurched, probably convey nothing more than the idea of going to church or getting to Heaven. But the former originally meant restoration of health, while the latter draws for its imagery on the notion of a captive gaining his freedom from slavery. Both thus speak of release from something unpleasant, and so these theologians in speaking of liberation are doing no more than updating Christianity's terminology into the language of today.

But what is it that the good news (gospel) of Jesus Christ brings release from? Is it something spiritual or something material or is this a false dichotomy? Is the message simply that, as Paul puts it, 'there is no condemnation in Christ Jesus'? Is it that there is no longer any need to prove oneself in God's eyes since the Cross has shown us that God loves and accepts us just as we are, however flawed? Or does the Bible imply something more? Liberation theology certainly claims so, and it is in this insistence that the Bible's message is about *the whole man* and *the whole society* that its significance lies. For, though it sometimes attempts to reinforce its argument by appeals to Marxism, this always remains subordinate to its attempt to reappropriate for today an aspect of the biblical message which it claims has been forgotten. This it detects pre-eminently in the imagery of the Exodus – oppressed slaves delivered by God into a 'land flowing with milk and honey'. That is what initiated Israel's faith and what gave the prophets their particular concern for the underprivileged in society, 'the orphan, the fatherless and the widow'. Of course they do not deny that individual charitable-giving has played a large role in the history of Christianity, but what they claim has been lost by the Church's failure to take the Old Testament with sufficient seriousness is the idea that God wishes the transformation of the whole of society and not just some individuals within it. That is why they think the legislation in the Pentateuch that was inspired by the prophets looks to a new order in society as a whole, not just the actions of some pious individuals within it.

In the space available all I can give is some brief indication of how a more detailed discussion of the merits of this approach might proceed. Accordingly, I shall mention one biblical and one non-biblical argument for and against in each case.

The obvious biblical argument in favour seems to me the basic correctness of what they say about the Old Testament. One need only think about the way in which God's involvement is always portrayed in terms of his relationship with the people as a whole rather than with particular individuals. Of course it has to be mediated through individuals, but their role is seen as essentially bound up with the future of the nation as a whole. So though the call to move to Palestine from distant Ur is addressed to an individual, Abraham, its significance is interpreted as the founding of the nation: 'Get thee out of thy country...and I will make of thee a great nation' (Gen. 12:1–2). Similarly, when things later go wrong in the relationship, the promise made through the prophets is that a remnant will be saved, not particular individuals. Indeed, so strong was this social conception of existence that the only form of immortality thought possible until very late in Old Testament writings (e.g. Dan. 12:2) was living through one's children. Instead, so far as the earlier period is concerned, 'the dead praise not the Lord, neither any that go down into silence' (Ps. 115:17) This strongly social conception of existence also resulted in a different, more profound conception of 'peace' than our own. For us peace means, at the least, absence of conflict, and, at most, mental tranquility. But the Hebrew *shalom* connotes complete wholeness – physical as well as spiritual, communal as well as individual. Often a better translation is 'abundance' or 'well-being', and in the redeemed community it must be a prosperity in which everyone can share: 'And they shall sit every man under his vine and under his fig tree; and none shall make them afraid' (Mic. 4:4).

But if the general tenor of the Old Testament pulls us to a more social, corporate view of salvation, so too does the history of the use of Christianity by the state. For it cannot be denied that, though it can take credit for numerous works of personal charity over the centuries, rather than encouraging social change, Christianity has often inhibited it. Too often has it been used as a means of simply reinforcing the existing social order. Though the French and Russian Revolutions were to produce numerous evils in their turn, this at least does much to explain the violence of their hostility to the Church of the time. The fault in fact set in very early. Already in the fourth century we find the church historian Eusebius celebrating the conversion of Constantine by repeatedly making the connection between his empire and God's. He introduces the relevant section by observing that 'then the God of all, the Supreme Governor of the whole universe, by his own will appointed Constantine. . . to be prince and sovereign.' Again, the victory over Licinius that finally established Constantine's absolute power is described in terms of 'taking God, the universal King. . . as guide and ally'. So an image that might have been used to offer a critique of all earthly power has in fact been turned into its endorsement. There is a similarly blatant expression in the Prayer for the Queen that is to be found in the 1662 Anglican *Book of Common Prayer*: 'O Lord. . . high and mighty, King of kings, Lord of lords, the only Ruler of princes, who dost from thy throne. . .' In Latin America even the Crucifixion has been used to reinforce and endorse the *status quo*. Jesus was held up as a model of passivity, and so instead of the peasants being encouraged to try to better their lot, religion was used to make it endurable. Salvation thus came to be seen as total acceptance of suffering. It is this fact which explains the extraordinary phenomenon (especially among the native Indian population) of ceremonial re-enactments of the Crucifixion, extending even to the use of real nails. It is perhaps therefore hardly surprising that Liberation theology, in reacting against such a tradition of passivity, almost totally ignores the Crucifixion, and instead takes the Exodus as its central symbol.

But if the above illustrates the sort of arguments, non-biblical as well as biblical, which might be used in support of its case, arguments can equally be found on the other side. A biblical critique might begin by attempting to contrast the general thrust of the New Testament with that of the Old. Jesus, though addressing himself to the outcasts of society – 'publicans and sinners' –, seems concerned about asserting their worth (their value in God's eyes) rather than in changing anything about their material status. Also, the way in which he voluntarily goes to the Cross rather than engaging in any form of resistance suggests that he was more concerned about a change in personal attitudes rather than in society as such. Certainly to judge by the earliest writings in the New Testament (from St Paul) one would be hard put to it to detect any hint that Jesus's teaching was taken to imply the end of the present social order. Indeed, as his letter to Philemon illustrates, Paul, though pleading that Philemon will treat his runaway slave Onesimus more like a brother, none the less does send him back to slavery, as the law required. Elsewhere too (cf. I Cor. 7:20–4) he urges slaves to be content with their lot.

Yet interpreting the Bible is seldom that simple. The way in which biblical scholarship might impinge on the answer we give can be well illustrated by what we make of what Jesus says in Luke's Gospel about the poor: 'How happy are you who are poor: yours is the kingdom of God', together with its corresponding woe: 'But alas for you who are rich; you are having your consolation now' (Luke 6:20 and 24). This is part of the material from Q that Luke uses, but intriguingly not only does Matthew in his parallel passage not have the woe, his is the better-known version of the beatitude and reads: 'Blessed are the poor in spirit; for theirs is the kingdom of heaven' (Matt. 5:3). In chapter 2 we saw that, where we can compare Matthew and Luke with their original source as in the case of Mark, it is Luke rather than Matthew who is found to display greater fidelity to his sources. So it would seem reasonable to suppose that in this case too Luke is more accurate in taking us back to what Jesus actually said. From such a conclusion we might then go on to argue that Jesus's message was after all essentially concerned with the transformation of society and that Matthew has unnecessarily spiritualized it. As further support we might note how in another beatitude Matthew's 'hunger and thirst after righteousness' replaces Luke's 'blessed are you who are hungry now' (cf. Matt. 5:6 and Luke 6:21).

But still the argument is not at an end. For by the time of Jesus 'the poor' had come to have almost a technical meaning. Just as the Hebrew word for 'peace' proved difficult to translate into English, so is the same true here. The word *anawim* meant not just materially poor but also humble in the sense of fully recognizing and living in dependence on God. One can see the beginning of the development of this usage already in the seventh-century BC prophet Zephaniah (cf. Zeph. 2:3 and 3:12). Indeed, the latter verse illustrates well the perils of translation with the Authorized Version's 'afflicted and poor people' contrasting nicely with 'the humble and lowly people' of the Jerusalem Bible, in much the same way as Luke contrasts with Matthew. Matthew can thus be seen as simply trying to bring this point out, however inadequately, rather than perverting the true heart of Jesus's message.

My example of a non-biblical argument against Liberation theology can be put more briefly. In recalling us to the strong social dimension of Old Testament teaching, such theologians assume that its social and material structures can continue to speak to us today. But that is an assumption which could be questioned. For ancient Israel was based on a simple agrarian economy, whereas our nations in the West have a complex, capitalist base. In the former case, since the total amount of wealth remains static, it is hard to see how great increases in wealth could be made without some form of exploitation, most obviously perhaps through the expropriation of land: whereas in a capitalist economy, based as it is on continuous growth, while exploitation can and does occur, it need not. For the additional wealth generated need not necessarily be at someone's expense, unless all profit is seen by definition as exploitative. It is this difference that explains why in our own society we think there is nothing wrong in the taking of interest, whereas in the Old Testament it is frequently condemned. For them, unlike for us, it practically always entailed still further reducing the plight of the poor.

Though my primary purpose here has been to characterize theological arguments rather than reach any definite conclusions, it would be quite wrong to leave Liberation theology on such a negative note. The two counter-arguments are in any case much weaker than they may initially have appeared. Matthew's 'poor in spirit' may be just as loyal to the teaching of Jesus, but this must not be allowed to disguise the fact that the word *anawim* still included in its meaning a reference to the materially poor. Jesus promises a blessing upon those who are both materially poor and spiritually reliant on God. In other words, the point is that same concern for *wholeness*, the integration of the material and the spiritual, to which, earlier, we saw Liberation theology pointing. The objection thus tells only against versions of the position which stress the material to the exclusion of the spiritual.

In a similar way, while to most of us the defence of capitalism in the developed world seems unproblematic, it is quite another matter when one encounters the extremes of poverty in the Third World. It is at this point that I come to the main reason why I cannot, and must not, leave Liberation theology on a negative note. For what I have hitherto failed to convey is anything of the sheer excitement existing among its practitioners. I am not thinking here of professional theologians, but of the ordinary members of the 'base ecclesial comunities' which have sprung up all over Latin America. These are groups of fifteen to twenty families who meet regularly for Bible study, and to discuss practical issues. Many will be very poor indeed and have endured years of drudgery. Yet all are now inspired by a new sense of confidence. For they know that the gospel is indeed good news, with God as much concerned for their material conditions as for their spiritual – in other words, for true wholeness of existence or, to use the more traditional language of theology, for salvation.

Feminist theology

Though Liberation theology began in Latin America, its influence has now spread to all parts of the world where a history of oppression is detected. In each case a key element in the

141

task has been seen as 'conscientization', that is, making people aware of their rights and responsibilities. For, where oppression has existed for centuries, part of the problem is apathy. Parents and grandparents have known only poverty and drudgery, and so the children too come to see that as their expected lot in life. Conscientization, feminist theologians maintain, must also be part of their aim: for the fact that millions of women appear content with their lot does not mean that through education they cannot be given access to a much richer, more fulfilled life.

But what is this 'conscientization' to involve? The range of issues confronting the contemporary Church is vast. Does the Bible with its predominance of male imagery (God as 'Father', 'He' and so forth) contribute to the subordination of women? If so, does it require rewriting, as some feminists have thought, or how is it to be used? What of the priesthood being confined to men? Does this suggest that leadership naturally only belongs to the man? In any case, apart from the physiological, are there any important differences between the sexes? Which are natural? Which merely the product of education and environment? For instance, is there any sense in which the mother is the more natural home-maker for the child? Or is this merely a long-standing convention? How are our conclusions about these issues to affect the practice of religion? Has the Virgin Mary's 'Be it unto me according to thy word' (Luke 1:38) been used in the past to suggest too passive a role-model for women? Does liturgical langugage need changing to reflect the equality of the sexes? Even this short list gives some idea of how radical and extensive the issues are.

Space permits discussion of only one topic here. Whereas the Bible has been one of the major factors contributing to the changed perspective of Liberation theology, this can scarcely be claimed for feminist theology. Instead, the pressures have overwhemingly come from secular culture. This is in no way to decry such pressures. As chapter 3 illustrated, the Church has been attempting to respond to contemporary culture ever since it moved out into the wider Greek and Roman world. But it does raise a question that many students of theology find deeply perplexing. What is the relation between the authority of the Bible and ideas drawn from secular culture? So I shall discuss that more limited issue here.

What needs to be conceded in the first place is not only that the Church's attitude to women in the past has been influenced by secular culture, but also that pressures for change have come from changes in the secular view. Let me mention here two of the more intellectual pressures for change.

First, there is our changed understanding of the facts of biology. The ovum was only discovered in 1827. While on the modern account both partners thus make an equal contribution, on the ancient view only the male semen was seen as performing an active role, with the woman's womb functioning as little more than a receptacle. According to Aristotelian biology (and adopted by the medieval Church), the menstrual blood was the basic matter which constituted the body of the child, but this was only brought to life by the semen which determined the child's true nature. As the Greek tragedian, Aeschylus, put it: 'She is no more than the nurse, as it were, of the newly conceived foetus. It is the male who is the author of its being.' Such 'facts', of course, could easily be used to reinforce a passive role for the female, and were so used.

Again, it was a nineteenth-century discovery which fundamentally undermined the use of the opening chapters of Genesis to reinforce female subordination. For, although a number of earlier theologians, including Origen and Kierkegaard, did not accept a literal interpretation, for several centuries, particularly since the Reformation, literalism had been firmly in the ascendancy. It took the discovery of the theory of evolution finally to break its power. At last Christians could perceive clearly that no particular significance should be attached to the fact that Eve was the first to partake of the fruits of the forbidden tree. That was just as well, as many an earlier theologian had used the story to endorse a subordinate position for women. For instance, Luther makes the following comment on the passage: 'The rule remains with the husband. . . The woman, on the other hand, is like a nail driven into the wall. She sits at home. . . In this way Eve is punished.'

But if the influence of secular culture in the past has been mixed (bad in the case of Aristotelian biology, good in the case of the theory of evolution), what are we to say today about the status of secular influences in relation to the authority of the Bible? Had the Bible already implicit within it a corrective, or is it more honest frankly to admit our debt to secular culture? Both courses involve difficulties, but these must be faced.

It would be hard to deny that some passages in the Bible are strongly subordinationist in tone (e.g. I Cor. 14:34–5; I Tim. 2:9–15). Against this are commonly set verses like Galatians 3:28: 'There is neither Jew nor Greek, neither slave nor free, neither male nor female, for all are one in Christ Jesus.' This can then be supplemented by mention of the occasional use of female imagery for God in the Old Testament (e.g. Isa. 49:15; 66:13); the way in which according to the Gospels it was a woman (Mary Magdalene) who was the first witness to Jesus's Resurrection; and the fact that some women seem to have exercised a major role in the early Church (Paul in Romans 16 calls Phoebe a deacon and Junia an apostle). Yet a nagging doubt remains about whether this is indeed the best way to proceed. Is there not a danger of pretending that the Bible is a book of the modern world when it is not? Thus if we take that same verse from Galatians, many scholars, drawing on Paul's thought as a whole, believe that what he had in mind was not the abolition of the priority of one over the other so much as the recognition of a mutual interdependency within a continuing hierarchy. Thus although the Gentile is to be converted as well as the Jew, the chosen race for Paul remains the Jews. Again, although the slave is to take the opportunity of freedom if it is given him, he is not to demand it but remain obedient within his given situation. So similarly, the argument runs, Paul intends to recognize the interdependency of man and woman but the priority remains with the man.

That at any rate is one plausible, more negative reading of the text that needs to be faced. The tendency has been for feminist theologians, the more they detect such a pattern, to withdraw further and further from orthodox Christianity. Rival feminist mythologies are then sometimes produced, referring to the Mother Goddess and so forth. For instance, Mary Daly's successive books present a picture more and more remote from orthodox Christianity.

144

But such moves are puzzling for two reasons. First, even if the language was originally subordinationist, this does not mean that we have to read it in this way today. The Bible is the book of the Christian community, not just a static document tied to an original meaning and significance. That is why questions of what the text originally meant and how it should be used today in practising the Christian faith are by no means the same thing. Though we now know that the familiar readings from the prophets were never intended to identify specific events in Jesus's life, that does not make their use in this way illegitimate, since from the standpoint of Christian faith Jesus can still be seen in just such a light – as the suffering servant, as the fulfilment of Israel's story, and so forth. So similarly here, it would be a case of Paul unwittingly speaking at a level which, centuries later, we could appropriate as part of the good news for mankind. But, secondly, the fact that some things are learnt from secular culture rather than the Bible need not be seen as derogatory to the latter. The Bible could still retain the status of being the most important statement of God's will and purposes for the human race. Rather, just as we can now see democracy as part of an equal regard for all – God has not favourites – without having to seek specific verses for biblical endorsement, so the same would be the case with regard to the status of women. The implications of Jesus's message included both, though we have needed the help of secular culture (which is also a divine creation) to make this clear to us. In short, even if Galatians 3 should be discovered to have been less profound in its original context than we usually think, the implications are much less traumatic than commonly supposed.

The liturgical movement

If Liberation theology was the recovery of a forgotten aspect of the Bible and feminist theology a learning from secular culture, my third and final example is a case of a recovery of lost perspectives from the history of the Church. It will depend on your age how aware you are of the changes that have occurred in the liturgies of the churches over the past twenty or more years. The transformation is at its most dramatic in the Roman Catholic Church which as a result of the Second Vatican Council (1962–5) moved almost overnight from its elaborate Latin Mass to the very simple vernacular liturgies that now characterize most Catholic churches. Several other denominations, including the Anglican Church, followed a very similar pattern in their reordering of the Communion Service and encouragement of the priest to face the people, use modern English and foster congregational participation. All theology is concerned with the existence of a Being greater than ourselves, upon whom Christians believe they depend for their existence and who gives their lives a meaningful pattern and structure. That fact is expressed in worship. So it is appropriate that our final example should consider briefly the theological significance of all the changes that have taken place in recent years, especially as these are the most dramatic since the Reformation.

Those who dislike change often complain of the Church being 'trendy' and altering 'the way things always have been'. But one of the advantages of a knowledge of the Church's history is the realization that it has always been in the process of change, adapting to new circumstances. The process is already at work in the New Testament itself. The early community moved its principal day of worship from the sabbath (Saturday) to Sunday, because that was the day of Jesus's Resurrection (cf. I Cor. 16:2; Acts 20:7). Again, the earlier tradition of having the Communion in the context of a meal with the bread at the beginning and the wine at the end, as reflected in I Corinthians 11, is eventually superseded in later accounts (e.g. Mark 14, 22–4) by the absence of an interval. Perhaps the occasion for this change was the very disrespectful behaviour of which Paul speaks: 'Everyone is in such a hurry to start his own supper that one person goes hungry, while another is getting drunk' (v. 21). The numerous further changes that then followed in the post-biblical period in fact came more slowly than often thought. So, for instance, even as late as 428 no special vestments were being worn by the clergy at Rome, and the saying of the Creed was only introduced there in 1014. The use of unleavened wafers, as distinct from ordinary bread, only started to come into general practice in the eleventh century and the elevation of the consecrated host at the beginning of the thirteenth. So, whatever the rebellious Archbishop Lefevre has said in claiming that only the post-Reformation form of the Mass from Pius V is valid, the Roman Catholic Church has much of the history of the pre-Reformation Church to draw upon in justifying its liturgical changes. Likewise the Protestant churches have become increasingly aware that in worship the Reformation was an over-reaction to the medieval Mass. 'The breaking of bread' would have been the normal form of worship in the earliest Christian communities and a relatively simple form of eucharistic worship was retained long into the post-biblical period.

Such a recovery of the Church's past has also helped in ecumenical relations as models for the liturgy have been sought in a common past. So, for instance, the Second Eucharistic Prayer of the Roman Mass and the Third Consecration Prayer of the Anglican liturgy are both heavily indebted to a prayer preserved by Hippolytus and dating from 215. But motives of course run deeper than just a love of the past or a new-found concern for ecumenical relations. The change can also be used to illustrate one of the central features of all theological endeavour: its need to resort to symbolism because of its central focus being in God who is not embodied like ourselves and so is vastly beyond our imaginings. If one then asks what the main change in the symbolism of the liturgy has been, there can be no doubt about the answer. The Second Vatican Council's *Constitution on the Liturgy* mentions the word 'participation' no less than twenty-six times, and there is no doubt that this is similarly reflected in what has taken place in other churches. Instead of the older model of us going towards God as passive observers either of the sacrament exposed (the elevated host) or of word preached, now it is a case of God coming among us and strengthening us for his mission in the world. Distant altars (at the east end of the church), at which the priest celebrated with his back to the people, have given place to tables set in their midst with the priest now standing behind as president. The whole orientation of the church is thus transformed. The movement is no more up to the altar and beyond to another world, but from the altar out towards the world and its sanctification.

Of course something is always lost in such changes, and there has perhaps been a loss of the sheer mysteriousness of God. But by way of compensation has come fresh awareness of the fact that the central act of the Christian faith, which the Eucharist celebrates ('eucharist' is simply the Greek word for thank-you), is about God having taken the initiative in Jesus to transform human lives. It is by symbolically participating in that life (as recalled in the service) that we too can become renewed and enriched by the transforming power of his Spirit.

I began this book by pleading that we take more seriously the attempts of primitive peoples to express their religious sensibilities through myths. It is appropriate therefore that I end it by stressing that, though I do not see the creation of new mythologies as an appropriate means of theological reflection in the twentieth century, it does none the less remain firmly a symbolic activity: one in which we will never succeed in capturing fully in our words and actions the boundless riches of its central concept, the source of all that is – God.

Glossary

An asterisk indicates that the term concerned is explained elsewhere in the Glossary; inverted commas, the nearest literal translation for the word being defined.

aetiological Type of myth* concerned to give an explanation of why a particular person or place has been so named.

Allah Muslim* name for God.

analytic philosophy The approach to philosophy currently dominant in the English-speaking world, which attempts to resolve problems by formal analysis of language and its implications, rather than by appeal to experience, as in the continental approach.

anthropomorphism Representing God as having human characteristics, as in J's* account of the Fall in Genesis 3:8 'And they heard the voice of the Lord God walking in the garden in the cool of the day.'

apocalyptic Type of literature concerned with the 'disclosure' of a forthcoming new age, often identified with the end of the world.

apocryphal Name given to a number of books written between Old Testament and New Testament times, and sometimes printed with them in the Bible, particularly in Roman Catholic versions.

Apostles' Creed   One of the two main creeds* in use within Christianity. A pious legend that it was the joint composition of the twelve apostles explains its name, but in fact it almost certainly dates from a creed produced at Rome in the second century AD. It is the creed most commonly used at all services apart from the Eucharist*.

atman   Nearest Hindu* equivalent of the western idea of the 'soul' or mind, of a person, but also used of the 'soul' of everything and in this sense equivalent to Brahman*.

atonement   Literally at-one-ment, the doctrine of the means whereby Jesus Christ brought about reconciliation between God and human beings.

avatar   In Hinduism* the 'descent' of a god to earth whereby he manifests himself in human or animal form. The most famous avatar of the god Vishnu* is as Krishna* in the *Bhagavadgita*. The concept is different from that of the Christian notion of Incarnation*, because the latter claims that God in Jesus not merely took on the form of man but actually became a man.

ayatollah   'Sign of God', term of respect for Iranian religious leaders, not much used in other parts of Shi'ite* Islam*.

Bhagavadgita   The 'Song (Gita) of the Lord (Bhagavat)', it is the best-known and most important of the Hindu* scriptures. It forms part of the sixth book of the great epic, the *Mahabharata*, but it is now commonly printed separately. The warrior Arjuna hesitates before battle and is enjoined by his charioteer (who turns out to be Krishna, an avatar* of the god Vishnu*) to follow the path of duty and devotion (*bhakti**).

bhakti   One of the three paths of salvation* in Hinduism, that of devoted love for a god, rather than ritual activity (*karma*) or spiritual knowledge (*jnana*).

Brahman   Hindu* term for the divine reality that is seen as pervading all things. Even the individual gods like Shiva* and Vishnu* are regarded as only aspects of this one divine, all-encompassing reality. The term should not be confused with *brahmin*, which is the name for the highest of the four castes within society and which provides Hinduism with its priests.

Brahman nirguna   The divine reality 'without attributes'. Because the divine reality is so vastly beyond our imaginings, Hindus claim that we can only properly talk of it being in itself 'not this' or 'not that', without assigning any positive attributes. If we want to say anything more, we must resort instead to talking in terms of a plurality of gods.

Buddha   Title meaning 'enlightened', and so used of someone who completely understands the nature of spiritual realities. Theravada* Buddhism claims that in our own world this has been true of only one person, Siddharta Gautama, the founder of Buddhism in the sixth century BC. For this reason 'Buddha' has become the most common way in the West of referring to Siddharta Gautama. However, the other main branch of Buddhism, Mahayana*, admits the existence of countless Buddhas and Bodhisattvas, the latter of whom have delayed their own nirvana* in order to help others.

caliph   Name given to the successive leaders of the Islamic world after the death of Muhammad* in AD 632; hence the name 'successor'. The minority Shi'ites* took a higher view of the office than the majority Sunnis*, regarding the earlier ones as divinely inspired imams*. In 1924 with the collapse of the Ottoman Empire the position was finally abolished.

Canaan   Ancient name for the land of Israel prior to its conquest by the Hebrews.

canon   Literally 'a measuring rod', and so used to describe the agreed authoritative scriptures of a particular religion.

Christ Though now used as a proper name, originally simply the Greek translation of the Jewish term 'Messiah', meaning 'the annointed one'. Biblical scholars now commonly distinguish between the historical 'Jesus' and the preached 'Christ'.

Christology Teaching about the significance of Christ.

Church fathers Name given to Christian writers of the first four or five centuries after the New Testament period, who by their authority ('father') gave definitive shape to the future form of Christian belief.

conscientization Giving people a consciousness or awareness of their true situation.

cosmological argument One of the traditional arguments for God's existence. It argues from the universality of causation (that every known event has a cause) to the conclusion that the only adequate termination of the causal question must be in a Being who by definition requires no such causal explanation. God, it is claimed, is such a Being since by definition he is the source of all that is and dependent on nothing.

creed Short statement of corporately held beliefs, usually recited publicly in the context of a service of worship. It takes two forms in Christianity, the Apostles* and the Nicene* Creed.

D Name given to one of the four sources of the Pentateuch* because its author was responsible for the Book of Deuteronomy. He (or his school) is also thought to have written the other history books that follow Deuteronomy in our present Bibles, up to the end of 2 Kings (but excluding Ruth).

Dead Sea Scrolls Scrolls discovered in eleven caves by the Dead Sea between 1947 and 1956, and belonging originally to a strict Essene community from nearby Qumran. They are of inestimable value in providing us with a better picture of Jewish views and expectations at the time of Jesus, as the material dates from between 250 BC and AD 68.

Diaspora The 'spreading out' of Jews throughout the known world began with the fall of the two kingdoms, first Israel in 722 BC and then Judah in 586 BC. Even after the restoration of Jerusalem in 539 BC, not all Jews who had been exiled returned. Trade as well as persecution played its part in this 'dispersion'. The two major revolts of the Jews against the Romans in AD 70 and AD 135 completed the process, since these resulted in the total destruction of the Jewish state, which ceased to exist except as a Diaspora until the re-creation of Israel in 1947.

doublet Two versions of the same incident or story.

dualism Any theory recognizing two completely independent realities, for example mind and matter or a good and an evil god.

E The second oldest of the four sources of the Pentateuch*, perhaps dating from the ninth century BC. So called because of the author's distinctive use of *Elohim* as his name for God.

ecumenical From a Greek word referring to the entire 'inhabited' world. Used (1) of the early Councils of the Church such as Nicaea in AD 325, in which the entire Church throughout the known world was represented, and (2) of modern movements towards improved relations between the various denominations that make up the world-wide Church.

Eightfold Path The last of the Buddha's* Four Noble Truths* and the means of achieving *nirvana**. The first two elements (Right Understanding and Right Resolve) involve understanding the Buddha's way and resolving to follow it. The next three concern a proper life-style: Right Speech is a commitment to the truth, while Right Action requires avoidance of harm to others and Right Livelihood an occupation compatible with these two objectives. The final three address themselves to our mental condition: with Right Effort we exclude the wrong sort of thoughts, Right Mindfulness ensures a proper awareness of what we are doing, while Right Concentration is concerned with the cultivation of an inner peace.

eschatology Teaching about the 'last things', so particularly about the end of the world. For discussion of whether the language is to be taken literally, see 'realized eschatology'.

Eucharist Also known as the Lord's Supper, Holy Communion and the Mass, the most important service of Christian worship in which 'thanks' are offered to God for what he has done through Jesus on the Cross.

evangelist Gospel writer, from the Greek word for gospel, *evangelion*.

Exile Sixth-century BC deportation of Jews to Babylonia; part of Diaspora*.

Filioque The clause in the western version of the Nicene* Creed* which speaks of the Spirit 'proceeding from the Father and the Son'. The inclusion of the phrase 'and the Son' was one of the causes which led to the split between eastern and western Christendom in AD 1054. The Orthodox* east objected to its inclusion on two grounds: (1) it had been done without the agreement of the whole Church; and (2) it seemed to imply a different understanding of the Trinity, that the Father was not the sole source of the other two persons' godhood.

form criticism The study of the form of a text in order to identify both the manner of, and the reasons for, its transmission, particularly at the oral stage. It has led to the identification of various types of short units which could easily be passed from mouth to mouth, such as pronouncement stories, and also to a concern with the life-setting, the continued relevance which ensured the story's survival.

foundationalism The philosophical view that claims to knowledge are only justified if they can be shown to be either derivable from certain foundational claims or themselves foundational, in which case they must either be self-evidently true (e.g. 'Man is an animal') or incorrigible, that is, not liable to subsequent revision (e.g. 'It seems to me that I am seeing a printed page'.)

Four Noble Truths The analysis of suffering taught by Buddha*. The first truth is that all life involves pain, the second that the cause of this suffering is desire or craving, the third that release is possible from such craving through detachment from the senses, and the fourth is the Eightfold Path* which outlines the steps which must be taken to secure this end.

fundamentalism Belief that a sacred text is totally without error. It is usually combined with the conviction that no supplementary authority is required to guide the believer's faith and practice. In Christianity fundamentalism is particularly prominent in Evangelical sects and in Islam* among those who attack the authority of later tradition and insist upon a very literalistic application of the Quran*.

Gnosticism An approach to religion which offers salvation* through 'knowledge'. Its origins are disputed. It may possibly be pre-Christian but certainly in its Christian form in the first three centuries AD it posed a major threat to orthodox* Christianity. In contrast to the latter's world-affirming doctrine of the Incarnation* it offered knowledge of frequently very elaborate mythological structures as a way of the soul escaping from its present captive state in this hostile world.

gospel Corruption of Old English words 'god' meaning 'good' and 'spel' meaning 'news': thus literal translation of Greek New Testament word for 'good news'.

grace God's 'good favour' or kindly disposition towards us, which results in his individual acts of grace to us. When human beings respond in gratitude, they sometimes say a 'grace' of thanksgiving, as for instance before a meal.

Hasidism Movement within Judaism* that began in the eighteenth century and, reached its peak in the middle of the nineteenth century when almost half the Jews of eastern Europe subscribed to it. A popularized form of the mystical Kabbalah*, it placed experience and worship above ritual and law, and often took ecstatic forms in chanting and dancing.

Hellenistic Term used to describe the culture of the eastern half of the Roman Empire, in which the principal common language was Greek rather than Latin, thanks to the conquest of this part of the world by Alexander the Great (356-323 BC).

Hinduism A name coined by Europeans to describe the religion of the Hindus, that is, those who live 'beyond the Indus river' in India.

Holocaust Commonest type of sacrifice in Old Testament times when the sacrificial animal was 'burnt in its entirety' (Lev. 1); now used to describe the Nazi persecution of the Jews when almost the whole people was destroyed (six million).

host The consecrated bread of the Eucharist*. From the Latin *hostia* meaning 'victim', the term is intended to recall Jesus' sacrifice on the Cross, and to emphasise his present intercessory role on our behalf.

icon Type of religious picture venerated by Orthodox* Christians. They are considered to be not just pictures but also in some sense to participate in the reality they are trying to represent.

imam (1) The person who leads worship in a mosque; he is not a priest or minister as in Christian worship, but an ordinary layman. (2) Among Shi'ites* the name for those first few caliphs* or leaders whom they regarded as divinely inspired. Shi'ites also await the return of one last such figure, known as the Mahdi.

immanence The idea of God or the divine 'remaining within' the world, and so at work from inside rather than outside it. Hinduism* for instance stresses the immanence of Brahman* in all things.

Incarnation Doctrine that God 'took on flesh', that he became a human being in Jesus Christ: in other words, the claim that God and Jesus are in certain senses one and the same Being.

indulgence The remission by the Church on earth of a penalty that is otherwise due for sin.

Islam 'Submission' or 'surrender' to God, the proper name for the religion of those who follow the teaching of the Quran*. A word with the same meaning – Muslim* – is used to describe a follower of this religion.

J The earliest of the four sources of the Pentateuch*, probably dating from the reigns of David and Solomon in the tenth century BC. The source is so called because of the author's use of Yahweh (traditionally transliterated as Jehovah) as his name for God.

Jesuits Popular name for the Society of Jesus founded by St Ignatius Loyola in 1534. To the normal religious vows was added the obligation to go wherever they were sent by the Pope to win souls. Their quasi-military constitution under a General ensured that they were one of the most effective forces in the Counter-Reformation.

Judaism The term used of the form of the Jewish faith in which the notion of law is particularly stressed and which developed from the sixth century BC onwards after the collapse of national independence. Scholars sometimes mark the distinction by speaking of the earlier Old Testament period as belonging to the Hebrews.

justification by faith The claim, particularly associated with Martin Luther (1483-1546), that one is 'justified' or 'deemed righteous' in God's eyes, not by virtue of any good acts of one' own, but solely by virtue of faith in the good God himself has done on the Cross.

Kabbalah   The 'received tradition' of Jewish mysticism*, it has had a very long continuous history from perhaps the sixth century AD. The Bible is interpreted as having an esoteric meaning with the world emanating out of God as in Hinduism* rather than being created out of nothing as in mainstream Judaism*.

Koran   See Quran.

Krishna   An avatar* of the god Vishnu*. The most religiously significant part of his story is told in the *Bhagavad-gita*.

Liberation theology   Theological movement originating in Latin America in the late 1960s, which has as its leading idea the liberation of people from oppressive structures.

lingam   Stone phallus used to symbolize the creativity of Shiva*, of which there are millions all over India. In contrast to what the symbol might suggest in the West, they can even be worn round the neck by a sect like the Lingayata to represent their ideals of strict moral reform.

liturgical movement   Though sometimes used of a reform movement within Roman Catholicism already in existence at the beginning of the twentieth century, nowadays the term primarily refers to initiatives within all the denominations to increase lay involvement in worship. Within the Roman Catholic Church the movement was given a very strong impetus by the reforms of the Second Vatican Council (1962–5).

liturgy   A formal service of worship.

Logos   Greek not only for 'word' but also for 'account' or 'explanation'; hence its use in both Stoicism* and Christianity to identify the explanatory key to understanding the nature of reality – in Christianity's case, Jesus Christ.

Mahabharata   Hindu* epic and longest poem in the world (100,000 verses), it has a complicated plot about the battles between two branches of a family. Its religious interest lies mainly in the role of Krishna*, one of the avatars* of Vishnu*.

Mahayana   'The great vehicle' of salvation*. Though it now has more adherents than the other major branch of Buddhism, Theravada*, it seems only to have come to prominence at about the time of Christ, five centuries after the Buddha's* death. Variants are to be found in Tibet, China, Korea, Japan and Vietnam. It resembles Hinduism* more than Theravada* and also has closer parallels with Christianity, for instance in notions like grace and faith.

marabout   Term used within Islam* for a saint or one of his family, particularly in north Africa where they once exercised a major role in arbitrating family and tribal disputes.

Marcan priority   The claim that Mark was the first of the four Gospels to be written.

maya   Hindu* view of the visible world as 'illusion'. However, it is important to note that this is not the same things as hallucination. Rather, the claim is that there really is something there – the divine unity that encompasses all things – but it is concealed behind the multiplicity of appearances.

Methodism   Branch of Christianity that had its roots in the teaching of the Anglican John Wesley (1703–91). Though his conversion experience dates from 1738, the term 'Methodist' was already in use by then to describe what his contemporaries regarded as his over-scrupulous behaviour.

monistic   View that only one thing exists. Some versions of Hinduism* are pantheistic*, asserting that Brahman* is in everything, while others are monistic, claiming that Brahman simply is everything. A monistic experience involves a feeling of complete identity with what might otherwise have been described as the object of the experience.

monotheism   The belief that there is only one God.

Muhammad   The founder of Islam*. The revelations he experienced began when he was about forty in AD 610 and continued to his death in 632. Though these now constitute the Quran*, it is important to note that it is rude to call a follower of Islam a 'Mohammadan'. This is because unlike Christ he is accorded no divine honours. He regarded himself as simply the last of the prophets (of whom Jesus was one).

Muslim   The proper term to use in describing a follower of Islam*. It also has a similar meaning – someone 'submissive to God'.

mysticism   Used in wide variety of different senses, but particularly to refer to direct, personal experience of God. The subject perceives himself as either in complete union with God, though still distinct from him, or as so completely united as to be identical with him. The latter type of experience is called monistic*.

myth   A story whose value and truth content is to be found in what it symbolizes rather than in its literal meaning.

natural religion   Expressions of religion that derive their understanding of God from the natural world as God's creation.

natural theology   In contrast to revealed theology*, conceptions of God derived from the nature of the world, as in arguments for the existence of God in the philosophy of religion.

Nicene Creed Christian creed* agreed at the first ecu-
menical* Council of Nicaea in AD 325, and recited by most
Christian denominations in the context of their Eucharist*
or Communion service.

nirguna See *Brahman nirguna.*

nirvana Ultimate Buddhist goal, often misunderstood as
meaning total 'extinction'. This is what the world literally
means, but what is intended is only the extinction of all
craving and desire, and thus the bliss that results.

original sin The inclination of human beings towards sin
that is present even before they commit some actual sin. The
expression is used today not to refer to an event in the distant
historical past (the Fall of Adam) but to those social and
psychological elements in our make-up which already
predispose us towards sin.

orthodox Having the 'right belief' in terms of the established traditions of a particular religion.

Orthodox (when written with a capital letter) (1) In a
Christian context this refers to the form of Christianity
found in most of eastern Europe and which separated itself
from Rome in AD 1054; (2) Orthodox Judaism is that part
of Judaism* which maintains all the traditional laws and
rituals, including the food laws, unlike Reform* or Liberal
Judaism.

Oxford Movement Reforming movement within the
Church of England which dated its origins to 1833 and
which was particularly the work of Newman, Keble and
Pusey, all one-time Fellows of Oriel College, Oxford. It was
concerned to establish a more Catholic conception of the
Church in its doctrine and worship, and in the latter half of
the nineteenth century this led to the beautifying of many
churches. Those who continue this tradition today are called
Anglo-Catholics.

P One of the four sources of the Pentateuch*, probably written not long after the fall of the southern kingdom in 586 BC; so called because of the author's strong interest in priestly matters such as forms of worship.

Pali canon While Hindu* scriptures are written in Sanskrit, those of Theravada* Buddhists are written in Pali; hence the name for this canon* of sacred Buddhist writings. They include discourse attributed to the Buddha*, though they were not finally committed to writing until the first century BC in Sri Lanka.

pantheistic Belief that 'God is in everything'.

papal infallibility The doctrine first promulgated in 1870 at the First Vatican Council that the Pope cannot err when he is speaking under certain conditions about faith and morals. This has only happened once since then, in 1950 when Pius XII declared it an article of faith that the Virgin Mary had been assumed bodily to Heaven at her death.

parallelism Characteristic of Hebrew poetry in which the thought of one line is repeated in very similar terms in the next (though in some translations both are printed as a single verse). Psalm 114 exhibits the form throughout:

> The sea fled at the sight,
> the Jordan stopped flowing,
> the mountains skipped like rams,
> and like lambs, the hills.
> (Psalm 114: 3–4).

patristic Of the Church 'fathers'*, and so used of the period of the early, post-New Testament Church, and of those theologians whose ideas were definitive in determining the future shape of Christian belief, for example St Augustine (AD 354–430).

Pentateuch From the Greek, meaning the first 'five books' of the Bible. Genesis takes the story as far as the arrival of the chosen people in Egypt, while the other four books deal with Moses' organisation of their liberation from slavery. Modern source criticism* has detected four sources lying behind our present text, J*, E*, D* and P*.

Platonism Probably the most influential school of philosophical thought in the ancient world. It owed its origins to Plato (427–347 BC), but took a number of different forms in the early Christian period, known as Middle and Neo-Platonism. But what characterized every variant was the conviction that knowledge was only possible through awareness of another, transcedent* world, and that any direct and immediate relation between the divine and this world was impossible.

polytheistic Belief in more than one god.

Prithivi 'The broad', the name for the earth in the *Vedas** and so personified in Hinduism* as the goddess who is earth mother of all things.

puja An act of worship particularly associated with *bhakti** Hinduism* in which one performs various acts before a Temple statue or a household god in order to symbolize one's devotion to the deity concerned. These may include washing and dressing the statue, as well as offering flowers, incense and some food.

purgatory Intermediate state to which those already destined for heaven go in order to be first purified of their sins or residual sinful character.

Q One of the two main sources for the Gospel of Matthew, and Luke, it is so named from the German word for source, *Quelle*. It consists almost exclusively of the teaching of Jesus rather than incidents from his life.

Quran The sacred text of Islam*. This is now the standard spelling, which has taken the place of the earlier 'Koran'.

It consists entirely of revelations given to the prophet Muhammad*.

Ramadan The month of fasting in the Islamic* calendar, during which nothing may be eaten or drunk until nightfall. The Quran* associates the period with the time during which Muhammad* first began to receive his revelations*

Ramayana Long Hindu* epic written about the time of Jesus, that tells the story of Rama, one of the avatars* of Vishnu*.

realized eschatology A term coined by the British New Testament scholar C. H. Dodd in his *The Parables of the Kingdom* (1935) to suggest that, though Jesus couched his message in the language and imagery of a future, impending Kingdom, his intention was to refer to a present reality that began in the here and now through his own person.

realizing eschatology A more recent suggestion than the preceding, which, though conceding that there is a future reference in Jesus' talk of the Kingdom, denies that he had any firm convictions about its imminence.

redaction criticism The attempt to identify the 'editorial' principles operating behind an evangelist's* arrangement of his material as a whole and the manner of its presentation, in particular the reasons lying behind the way he uses his sources.

reductionism The claim that one form of explanation is reducible to, and wholly explicable by, the laws of another more basic form of explanation. So, for example, it used to be a common claim that all sociological explanation could be reduced to an account exclusively in terms of individuals (psychology), and that this account in terms of individual human motivation (psychology) can be further reduced to an explanation exclusively in terms of physiological or biological drives, and so forth. In the case of religion one instance would be the assertion that religious experience (which claims to be an experience of God) is only really an expression of inner psychological needs.

Reform Judaism The other major branch of Judaism* besides Orthodoxy*, which had its origins in the early nineteenth century. The detailed, permanently binding law of Orthodoxy was rejected, the equality of the sexes accepted, and languages other than Hebrew introduced into the worship of the synagogue.

remnant motif Recurring idea in the Old Testament that, though the majority of the nation might perish or reject God, his purposes and promises would still be fulfilled through the loyality of a minority – the remnant.

revealed theology What has been disclosed about God through a religion's sacred text.

revelation The 'unveiling' or disclosing of God. Because God is its creator, some would see this as already taking place in the natural world, while others would wish to confine the word to what has been disclosed in a particular religion's sacred text.

salvation The two roots of the word suggest both being delivered from something unpleasant and being made whole or healthy. This suggests (what is in fact the case) that religions which stress salvation should offer both a diagnosis of what is wrong and the means of securing wholeness or health. It is important to add that not all forms of religion are religions of salvation. Some like Hinduism or the religion of the Greeks and Romans show themselves much more concerned to give a meaning and pattern to an already existing situation.

Sangha Order of monks founded by Buddha* himself, and so possibly the world's oldest religious order. They play a stronger role in Theravada* than in Mahayana* Buddhism because of the former's stress on a personal search for enlightenment rather than on notions of mutal help and the grace* of those much further advanced on the path than oneself, as in the latter. Temporary membership varying from three months to one year is commonly used as a form of marriage preparation.

scholastic philosophy The term used to describe the essentially philosophical approach to religious issues in much medieval writing, and which has continued to influence Roman Catholic thought to the present day, especially through the writings of St Thomas Aquinas (1225–1274). It takes its name from the fact that many of the important earlier figures taught in cathedral schools, the predecessors of our present universities.

Shema The confession of faith used by Jews both in public worship and in their private prayers. It consists of Deut. 6: 4–9 and 11: 13–21 and Num. 15: 37–41. It affirms the unity of God, his love for Israel and the worshipper's resolve to keep his commandments.

Shi'ite The minority group within Islam* who date their origins from their loyalty to Ali, the caliph* assassinated thirty years after Muhammad's* death. The word means 'the party of Ali'. They have a more charismatic understanding of authority than the majority Sunnis*, and are strongest in Iran, Iraq and Pakistan.

Shiva One of the two principal gods of Hinduism*, whose worship is particularly popular in southern India. As a god of fertility and creativity one of his symbols is the lingam*, while he is also represented as Lord of the Dance, in which he both creates and destroys. Perhaps because destruction is also seen as bringing with it the possibility of creativity, he is also associated with asceticism.

source criticism The attempt to detect sources, oral or written, lying behind our present biblical documents. The existence of 'joins' or artificial links in the narrative, as well as internal inconsistencies, are held to support the postulation of such sources. Characteristic features of style and recurring themes can then be used to distinguish between the sources.

Spirit christology An account of Christ's work and persons which assign a key role to the Holy Spirit. This is particularly prominent in Luke's Gospel.

Stoicism A philosophical school founded by Zeno in the third century BC. It is a form of materialistic pantheism*. The divine (the Logos*) is immanent* in all things, directing the world, and has no existence apart from it. Our duty lies in aligning ourselves with the direction of history already determined by this divine principle.

Sufi The mystical* movement within Islam* which has taken both orthodox* and heretical forms. In the latter it resembles the pantheistic* or monistic* tendencies within Hinduism*, while the influential theologian and philosopher Al-Ghazali (d.1111) did much to ensure its general acceptability within orthodoxy*.

Sunni By far the larger of the two main branches of Islam* (over 80 per cent). Meaning 'custom', it assigns a legitimate role to tradition as well as to the Quran*.

Synoptic Gospels Name given to the Gospels of Matthew, Mark and Luke because they were observed to share a similar perspective, in a way that the Fourth Gospel (John) does not. This is now commonly explained by the fact that Matthew and Luke have used Mark and one other source Q*, in the formation of their own accounts.

Tantrism A movement within both Hinduism* and Buddhism which attempts to use unorthodox means as a way of obtaining the religious goal. One instance of this is shock therapy, whereby the initiate is encouraged to do forbidden things such as eat meat or drink alcohol, as a way of breaking down traditional inhibitions and opening the path to new spiritual forces. Again, the sexual act is seen as a religious activity in which the male identifies with the god Shiva* and his partner with the god's spouse or Shakti, as a way of re-enacting the ecstatic union between the divine and the world which in fact already exists, according to Hinduism*, behind all the multiplicity of appearances.

theistic Belief in a personal God as the source of all reality. Buddhism is not a theistic religion because, though it acknowledges the existence of gods in other worlds, it accords them no real importance. Hinduism, on the other hand, can sometimes take a theistic form, but more commonly Brahman* is interpreted impersonally, in either a pantheistic* or a monistic* direction. Christianity, Islam and Judaisms, however, are all incontestably theistic religions.

Theravada 'The doctrine of the elders', the older but now smaller branch of Buddhism that is to be found mainly in South-East Asia (Sri Lanka, Burma, Thailand, Cambodia and Laos). By Mahayana* Buddhism it is called 'Hinayana' or 'small vehicle' because it is seen as involving a self-centred pursuit of enlightenment, in contrast to its own position which requires full enlightenment to be delayed so that one can help others.

Torah Name given by Jews to the 'teaching', particularly on law, as contained in the first five books of the Bible.

transcendent God as 'beyond' and outside the world, and not dependent on it. Of all the world religions Islam* has the most transcendent account of the divine, Hinduism* the most immanent*. What makes Islam's account the most transcendent is the way in which it is least prepared to admit that God could be affected by anything that happens in the world. Christianity with its doctrine of the Incarnation* lies somewhere in between.

transubstantiation   The conversion of the substance of the bread and wine in the Eucharist* into the Body and Blood of Christ, with only the outward appearances of bread and wine remaining. It was declared a doctrine of the Church in AD 1215 and remains the official Roman Catholic view of what happens.

Umayyad   The first dynasty of Sunni* caliphs* or leaders of Islam* who, ruling from Damascus (AD 661–750), succeeded in extending their empire as far as France.

Upanishads   Sacred Hindu* texts, of which thirteen are regarded as particularly important. Their main theme is that Brahman* is the supreme reality, the world we perceive mere illusion or *maya**, and that our own *atman** or soul is ultimately identical with, or at the very least closely related to, Brahman. Disputes over the last point led to the rival philosophical schools of Shankara (monistic*), or Ramanuja (moderate non-dualist) and Madhva (dualist*).

Vedas   The most ancient of the Hindu* scriptures, composed mainly of hymns in honour of the gods. Though surviving manuscripts date only from the fourteenth century AD, they were probably composed around 1000 BC and preserved simply by memory.

via negativa   'The negative way', a view within Christianity that one can only properly say what God is not, all positive descriptions being inadequate, or at most image or metaphor. Similar ideas are also found in other world religions: for a Hindu version, see *Brahman nirguna**.

Vishnu   One of the two principal gods worshipped within Hinduism*, best known for two of his avatars* as Rama and Krishna*. His cult is particularly prominent in northern and central India.

Wisdom literature   Name given to biblical literature which particularly appeals to human reason and experience rather than divine initiative and revelation*. Job, Proverb and Ecclesiastes are obvious examples, as is Ecclesiasticus (also known as Sirach) from the Apocrypha*.

Zeus   Principal god of the ancient Greek pantheon.

Further Reading

(All the books listed are relatively inexpensive paperbacks.)

CHAPTER 1

I know of no easy books about the nature of religion in general. Dermot Lane's *The Experience of God* (Paulist Press, 1981) raises some of the issues at the right introductory level, but has the disadvantage of assuming a Roman Catholic readership. Thomas Munson's *The Challenge of Religion* (Duquesne University Press, 1985) is good, but one would need some philosophical competence to follow the argument.

The range of current approaches to myth is well illustrated by *Sacred Narrative*, edited by Alan Dundes (University of California Press, 1984). A good example of changing attitudes to classical myth is Jean-Pierre Vernant's *Myth and Society in Ancient Greece* (Methuen, 1982). Given the length of the Hindu sagas it is good to have available Jean-Claude Carrière's play *The Mahabharata* (Methuen, 1988), as well as William Buck's re-telling of both this epic and *The Rāmayana* (University of California Press, 1981).

There is no shortage of books about comparative religion. A good introductory survey of the practice of the major religions is W. Owen Cole's *Six Religions in the Twentieth Century* (Hulton Educational Publications, 1984), while if one wants greater detail Ninian Smart's *The Religious Experience of Mankind* (Collins, 1971) is ideal. A useful reference aid is *A Handbook of Living Religions*, edited by John Hinnells (Penguin, 1984). All major sacred texts are readily available in Penguin Classics. In attempting to understand individual religions other than Christianity, personally I have found the following the most useful: K. M. Sen's *Hinduism* (Penguin, 1961), Nicholas de Lange's *Judaism* (Oxford University Press, 1986), Christmas Humphries's *Buddhism* (Penguin 1962) and Seyyed Hossein Nasr's *Ideals and Realities of Islam* (Unwin, 1979). Since those from a Christian background often find Hinduism the most difficult of these religions to understand, it is good also to have available VP (Hemant) Kanitkar's *We are Hindus* (Saint Andrew's Press, 1987) from a Hindu living in Britain and Bede Griffith's *The Cosmic Revelation* (Collins, 1983) from a Catholic monk who has run an ashram (prayer centre) for more than twenty-five years in India. In considering how the different religions might assess each other, preliminary thoughts will be aided by Geoffrey Parrinder's *Comparative Religion* (Sheldon, 1976) and Eric Sharpe's *Faith Meets Faith* (SCM, 1977).

Psychology of religion is well-served by Robert Thouless's *An Introduction to the Psychology of Religion* (Cambridge University Press, 1971) and Laurence Brown's *The Psychology of Religion: An introduction* (SPCK, 1988). Bruno Bettelheim writes on the meaning and importance of fairy tales in *The Uses of Enchantment* (Penguin, 1978). For those .particularly interested in religious experience in the contemporary world David Hay's *Exploring Inner Space* (Penguin, 1982) makes fascinating reading.

Currently there seems to be more interest in the sociology than in the psychology of religion. Here Robin Gill provides an excellent selection of both classical texts and its application to various aspects of theology in *Theology and Sociology: A reader* (Geoffrey Chapman, 1987). Richard Gombrich uses sociology to explore the origins and development of *Theravada Buddhism* (Routledge & Kegan Paul, 1988), while the application of sociological techniques to the history of Islam finds a powerful exponent in Ernest Gellner's *Muslim Society* (Cambridge University Press, 1981).

CHAPTER 2

Etienne Charpentier's *How to Read the Old Testament* (SCM, 1981) is probably the liveliest introduction available to critical study of the Old Testament. Rather more obviously academic in approach but also good are Henry McKeating's *Studying the Old Testament* (Epworth, 1979) and *Beginning Old Testament Study*, edited by John Rogerson (SPCK, 1988). A good knowledge of the history of the period would be gained by reading *The Living World of the Old Testament* by Bernhard Anderson (Longman, 1988), while some acquaintance with the wide range of techniques currently being applied in Old Testament study could be gained from John Barton's *Reading the Old Testament* (Darton, Longman & Todd, 1984).

Charpentier has also provided a lively approach to New Testament study in *How to Read the New Testament* (SCM,1981). Christopher Tuckett's *Reading the New Testament* (SPCK,1987) and Raymond Collins's *Introduction to the New Testament* (SCM,1983) are more obviously academic, but both are rich in examples which makes for easier comprehension. Those worried about the impact of such criticism on the general reliability of the biblical accounts might try reading John Robinson's *Can we Trust the New Testament?* (Mowbray,1977) and James Dunn's *The Evidence for Jesus* (SCM, 1985), while the latter's *The Living Word* (SCM,1987) or James Barr's *Escaping from Fundamentalism* (SCM,1983) should prove particularly useful for those still trapped into thinking that there can and must be only one way of reading Scripture.

Gerd Theissen successfully uses the medium of a detective story in his *The Shadow of the Galilean* (Fortress, 1987) to offer a vivid picture of the social context into which Jesus was born. How the social context might have affected the writing of Mark's Gospel in Rome and Matthew's in Antioch is explored in *Antioch and Rome* by Raymond Brown and John Meier (Geoffrey Chapman, 1983). Most examples of redaction criticism tend to make for rather heavy reading, but lighter versions of the genre may be found in J. L. Houlden's *Backward into Light* (SCM,1987) and Eduard Schweizer's *Luke: A Challenge to Present Theology* (SPCK,1982). They provide an interesting contrast. For while the method leads Houlden towards uncompromising hostility towards Matthew's approach, Schweizer seems to have experienced a change of heart, with Luke's lack of theological precision (for example, no atonement theory) now being subsumed under a deeper theological purpose of producing an open invitation to the reader to experience Christ for oneself.

Because biblical scholars usually see themselves as exclusively historians rather than theologians, it is perhaps not surprising that there is very little discussion among them about the impact of their studies for the status of Jesus. The two books *The Myth of God Incarnate*, edited by J. Hick (SCM, 1977), and *The Truth of God Incarnate*, edited by M. Green, (Hodder & Stoughton, 1977) provide the two extremes in interpretation. But since the contributions to both volumes are very uneven, perhaps it is easier to look at a narrower issue first. Willi Marxsen and Gerald O'Collins are both distinguished New Testament scholars, but whereas the former in *The Resurrection of Jesus of Nazareth* (Fortress, 1970) offers a purely subjective interpretation of what happened, O'Collins in his *Jesus Risen* (Darton, Longman & Todd) insists on the objectivity of the event while not in the least disguising any of the historical problems involved.

CHAPTER 3

E. H. Carr's *What is History?* (Penguin, 2nd edition, 1987) can be used to get the reader thinking about the nature of history, especially the degree to which subjective interpretations play their part. This could then be usefully supplemented by Jaroslav Pelikan's *Jesus through the Centuries* (Harper & Row, 1985), with its fascinating account of the numerous different portraits of Jesus that have been offered at different historical periods in the life of the Church.

Henry Chadwick's *The Early Church* (Penguin, 1967) is a very readable account of the early period. Maurice Wiles provide a good introduction to some of the leading themes in the writings of *The Christian Fathers* (Hodder & Stoughton, 1966). G. L. Prestige's *Fathers and Heretics* (SPCK,1968) is more detailed, but has the compensation of very engaging portraits of some of the leading figures involved. In trying to come to grips with the period Robin Lane Fox's *Pagans and Christians* (Penguin, 1987) and Peter Brown's biography of *Augustine of Hippo* (Faber & Faber, 1967) are both quite outstanding. The major Christian historian of the time was

Eusebius. It is a very rewarding exercise to read his *History of the Church* (Penguin, 1965) shortly after one has read a modern introductory work like that of Chadwick. The most obvious differences between our own age and his will not be long in emerging.

Christopher Brooke's *The Twelfth Century Renaissance* (Thames & Hudson, 1969) will help to set the Middle Ages in a more positive light. Bernard Hamilton's *Religion in the Medieval West* (Edward Arnold, 1986) answers in a very readable way all the basic questions one is likely to want to raise, while Emmanuel Le Roy Ladurie's *Montaillou* (Penguin, 1980) with its fascinating portrayal of life in a medieval village has justifiably become a best-seller. Novels are not always to be despised as a point of entry towards better understanding a period, and in this case two medievalists have also successfully tried their hand at writing novels. Helen Waddell's *Peter Abelard* (Collins, 1977) tells the story of one of the age's most distinguished theologians, while Umberto Eco's *The Name of the Rose* (Penguin, 1984), as well as being an exciting detective story, is full of insights into the nature of life in fourteenth-century Europe.

A. G. Dickens's *The English Reformation* (Fontana, 1967) and G. R. Elton's *Reformation Europe* (Fontana, 1963) are still extremely useful in providing the basic background and history of the Reformation, but now need to be supplemented by the changing perspective brought about by books like J. J. Scarisbrick's *The Reformation and the English People* (Basil Blackwell, 1984) and John Bossy's *Christianity in the West 1400–1700* (Oxford University Press, 1985). Alister McGrath's *Reformation Thought* (Basil Blackwell, 1988) summarizes the most recent assessments of the intellectual origins of the Reformation, while Keith Thomas provides us with valuable insights into the reasons for increased interest in witchcraft in his *Religion and the Decline of Magic* (Penguin, 1973).

For the modern period Hugh McLeod's *Religion and the People of Western Europe 1789–1970* (Oxford University Press, 1981) is a good guide, while those more narrowly interested in Britain might try F. G. Worrall's *The Making of the Modern*

Church (Mowbray, 1988). The continuing debate about whether ecclesiastical history has escaped from its former confessional perspective is well illustrated by John Kent's *The Unacceptable Face: The modern Church in the eyes of the historian* (SCM, 1987).

CHAPTER 4

There are numerous introductions to the philosophy of religion available. The most accessible and well-balanced is from an agnostic, J. C. A. Gaskin's *The Quest for Eternity* (Penguin, 1984). Unfortunately there is still no easy introduction to the most recent debates. However, one can still get a good idea of the general character of Richard Swinburne's argument even if one confines oneself to the later, less technical chapters of his *The Existence of God* (Oxford University Press, 1979). Alvin Plantinga's definitive defence of his position has not yet been published, but a good impression can be gained from *Faith and Rationality*, edited by Alvin Plantinga and Nicholas Wolterstorff (University of Notre Dame Press, 1983). The best current attack on the rational credentials of Christianity comes from J. L. Mackie in his sarcastically entitled *The Miracle of Theism* (Oxford University Press, 1982).

There is no good survey of current trends in Roman Catholic theology, but Alisdair Heron is excellent in dealing with *A Century of Protestant Theology* (Lutterworth, 1980), or if something shorter and lighter is preferred from a major practioner of the art, try Jürgen Moltmann's *Theology Today* (SCM, 1988). Keith Clements has provided a good introduction to selected texts in his *Friedrich Schleiermacher: Pioneer of Modern Theology* (Collings, 1987). This is the first in a series entitled *Makers of Modern Theology*, all of which are likely to prove useful. Edited highlights from Karl Rahner are available in *A Rahner Reader* edited by Gerald McCool (Darton, Longman & Todd, 1975), and from Balthasar in *The von Balthasar Reader*, edited by M. Kehl and W. Loser (T. & T. Clark, 1982). John Bowden gives a good portrait of *Karl Barth: Theologian* (SCM, 1983), while Rahner briefly explains his own development in *I Remember* (SCM, 1988).

Introductions to Liberation theology could be provided by

either Leonardo and Clodovis Boff's *Introducing Liberation Theology* (Burns & Oates, 1987) or Rosino Gibellini's *The Liberation Theology Debate* (SCM, 1987). Gustavo Gutierrez's *A Theology of Liberation* (SCM, 1974) is the classic in the field, but probably before attempting to read any of the vast amount of theological literature now being produced, the reader would be best advised to gain some more detailed knowledge of the political situation in the countries concerned, for example through reading Philip Berryman's *The Religious Roots of Rebellion* (SCM,1984).

In my view balanced accounts of the implications of feminist theology are offered by Ann Loades in *Searching for Lost Coins* (SPCK, 1987) and Mary Hayter in *The New Eve in Christ* (SPCK, 1987). But of course the reader should be allowed to judge for her or himself and this can easily be done by comparing the views of Hayter and Loades with those of more radical feminists like Rosemary Radford Ruether in *Woman-guides: Readings towards a feminist theology* (Beacon Press, 1985) or Mary Daly in *Gyn/Ecology (Beacon Press, 1978)*.

A good short history of liturgy is given by Pierre Loret in *The Story of the Mass* (Liguori, 1982), while some of the more important questions being raised today are discussed in Jean Lebon's *How to Understand the Liturgy* (SCM, 1987). Both of these assume a Roman Catholic perspective. Alan Dunstan provides a useful introductory account from an Anglican point of view in *Interpreting Worship* (Mowbray, 1984). It would take too long to list possibilities for each of the major denominations. Instead let me refer the reader to a major ecumenical project *The Study of Liturgy*, edited by Cheslyn Jones, Geoffrey Wainwright and Edward Yarnold (SPCK, 1978), within whose pages one will find all one is likely to want to know.

Index

Index

8/6/9
22/6/4

230
B877i

15523

Brown, David